Rivers in American Life and Times

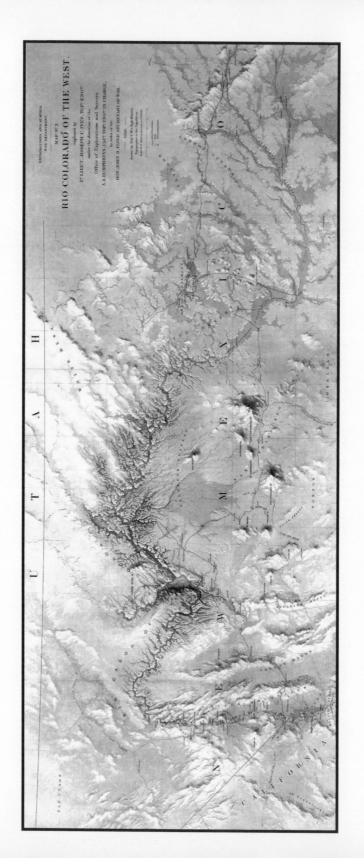

EXPLORATIONS AND SURVEYS.
WAR DEPARTMENT.

MAP N° 2

RIO COLORADO OF THE WEST.

explored by

1st LIEUT. JOSEPH C. IVES, TOP. ENG.
under the direction of the
Office of Explorations and Surveys
A.A. HUMPHREYS, CAPT. TOP. ENG. IN CHARGE,
by order of the
HON. JOHN B. FLOYD, SECRETARY OF WAR.
1858.

drawn by F.W. von Egloffstein.

The
COLORADO
RIVER

Tim McNeese

CHELSEA HOUSE
PUBLISHERS
A Haights Cross Communications Company
Philadelphia

FRONTIS: U.S. Army First Lieutenant Joseph C. Ives and his party from the Army Topographical Corps laid out the first relief map (shown here) of the Colorado River in the 1850s.

917.91
McNeese

CHELSEA HOUSE PUBLISHERS

VP, NEW PRODUCT DEVELOPMENT Sally Cheney
DIRECTOR OF PRODUCTION Kim Shinners
CREATIVE MANAGER Takeshi Takahashi
MANUFACTURING MANAGER Diann Grasse

Staff for THE COLORADO RIVER

EXECUTIVE EDITOR Lee Marcott
PRODUCTION EDITOR Megan Emery
PHOTO EDITOR Sarah Bloom
SERIES DESIGNER Keith Trego
COVER DESIGNER Keith Trego
LAYOUT 21st Century Publishing and Communications, Inc.

A Haights Cross Communications Company

www.chelseahouse.com

First Printing

9 8 7 6 5 4 3 2 1

Library of Congress Cataloging-in-Publication Data

McNeese, Tim.
   The Colorado River / by Tim McNeese.
      p. cm.—(Rivers in American life and times)
Includes index.
   ISBN 0-7910-7726-8—ISBN 0-7910-8006-4 (pbk.)
   1. Colorado River (Colo.-Mexico)—History—Juvenile literature. I. Title.
II. Series.
F788.M33 2004
979.1'3—dc22

                                                    2004000314

CONTENTS

1

The Great
Southwestern River

Despite running through some of the most extraordinary scenery found in the American West, the Colorado River is not known as a river of superlatives. Its length, just short of 1,500 miles, hardly qualifies the Colorado as America's longest river. (The Missouri River is at least 1,000 miles longer). Nevertheless, with 1,360 miles of the Colorado running through the United States, it is the nation's fifth longest. It is not the widest or even the wildest, although its canyon courses and narrow whitewater rapids draw some of the most ardent of river rafters. This great western river does not carry the greatest volume of water nor does it have the most dams. Yet it is the most important river of the entire American Southwest. Without the use of the waters of the Colorado, whole modern-day communities in the West, from Phoenix to Tucson to Las Vegas, would likely never survive.

The Colorado River Basin, which includes many tributary rivers, drains the portion of the American West that includes southwestern Wyoming and western Colorado, parts of California, Utah, Nevada, New Mexico, and nearly all of Arizona. Three out of every four square miles of the river's basin lands are owned by the United States government, comprising national parks, forests, and Indian reservation lands. Along 1,000 miles of the Colorado's course, the landscape has been scarred by the endless flow of this ancient river, resulting in the carving of many spectacular gorges and canyons. A half dozen or so massive and powerfully beautiful canyons, including the Marble, Black, Boulder, Topok, and the greatest of all deep gorges in the world, the Grand Canyon, have been formed by the waters of the Colorado. This super-sized canyon extends from the mouth of the Paria River, which flows southwest from Utah's Bryce Canyon and joins the Colorado to Grand Wash Stream just south of the central Utah-Arizona border. There, the river turns sharply south, forming the boundary between Arizona and Nevada.

The water that feeds the forceful Colorado comes from its many tributaries, including the Dirty Devil, Escalante, Green, Kanab, Paria, and Virgin, which flow into the upper and middle

The thousand miles of landscape along the Colorado River have been shaped and scarred by the river's flow over time. These sandstone narrows were carved by the river within the Grand Canyon, the most spectacular of the several gorges formed by the Colorado.

legs of the Colorado from the west. Other western-flowing rivers—the Dolores, Gunnison, Little Colorado, and San Juan—feed the great western river from the east.

Today, the Colorado River follows its ancient channel as it flows through and along the borders of five American states: California, Arizona, Utah, Nevada, and, of course, Colorado. Its headwaters originate in the majestic peaks of the Rockies in Colorado's Rocky Mountain National Park, northwest of Denver. There is more to the geography of the Colorado than these five states, however. Major tributaries of the Colorado, including the Green River in Wyoming, which is geologically a continuation of the Colorado, and the San Juan, which runs through New Mexico, add to the states that rely on the waters of the Colorado River Basin. Along Colorado's southern border, shared by California and Arizona, the river flows into two Mexican states, Baja California and Sonora.

Although only a fraction of the Colorado's watershed drains into Mexico (2,000 of 244,000 square miles), the river supports a total of 25 million people in seven American and two Mexican states. Among those millions of water users are 32 American Indian tribal groups that live on various reservations. In addition, the hydroelectric power generated by the Colorado River and its tributaries supplies 30 million people with electrical power.

Despite the Colorado River's modern-day contributions to the progress and survival of urban centers in the Southwest, the great desert river has flowed for tens of thousands of years, largely unchanged through eons of history.

Throughout its history, the Colorado River has been shaped by its unique geography. Many of the rivers in the United States flow in a given direction because of their proximity to various mountain ranges. In the case of the Rocky Mountains, the tallest mountain chain in North America, rivers flow from glacial peaks, either toward the Mississippi River to the east or the Pacific Coast to the west, according to their situation relative to the Continental Divide. The tallest spine of the Rockies forms this continental demarcation line, which runs north and south for 3,000 miles and spans Canada, the United States, and Mexico. Because the Colorado lies on the western side of the

Continental Divide, the river flows across the arid, desert lands of the Southwest.

According to geologists, the river was originally formed millions of years ago when forces deep beneath the earth's crust, centered in the general area of northern Arizona, slowly forced themselves upward and created a series of upheavals across the landscape. These upward thrusts pushed the earth's surface up several miles, causing the formation of the Rocky Mountain chain. Two distinct drainage systems—the Hualapai and the Ancestral Colorado—were begun and have developed over geologic time. The two systems were separated by a great plateau—the Kaibab Plateau—which stood only a few thousand feet above sea level. At that time, the Grand Canyon was nowhere in sight.

Over the millennium, as the Kaibab continued to rise, the Hualapai drainage system "cut back into the plateau, thus establishing the pattern of flow of the future Colorado River through the western end of what is now Grand Canyon."[1] The course of the Ancestral Colorado River followed very closely the course of the modern-day Little Colorado, forming a giant lake called Lake Bidahochi, which some geologists believe flowed into the Rio Grand River basin. Oddly enough, the Little Colorado flows west but the Ancestral Colorado River flowed in the opposite direction.

As the upheaval of the earth's crust continued to make the landscape rise, Lake Bidahochi's bed tilted, eventually causing the Ancestral Colorado and the Hualapai drainage to merge. Then, on "one momentous day, the last remaining rocks that separated the two drainage systems were gone," allowing the waters of Lake Bidahochi to flow into the gap. The Little Colorado River began to flow in the opposite direction, and the river that would in time form the Grand Canyon began to take shape. Geologists estimate that the entire process, from the origins of the dual drainage systems to the merging of the Ancestral Colorado River and the Hualapai drainage—a process known as "river capture"—began approximately 10 million years ago and was completed 5 million years later.

Millions of years ago, the Colorado River began to shape what is now the Grand Canyon. Today, the Colorado cuts a 277-mile path through the Grand Canyon National Park in Arizona.

Throughout the millennium to follow and even during the period of "river capture," the Colorado River, as well as many of its tributaries, worked its way downward across the landscape of the American Southwest:

> Slowly, using the grinding and cutting tools of rock, gravel, and sand, it began to slice its way down into the great plateau, tearing it down, carrying it grain by grain to the sea. . . . The task began perhaps twelve million years ago, and the river has cut through nearly six thousand feet of the plateau.[2]

Geology, topography, and massive hydraulics had worked over an incredibly long period of time to create the great water system that modern humans would come to call the Colorado River Basin.

Although the landscape of the Colorado River Basin may have originated millions of years ago, the region has known human occupation for only thousands of years. Anthropologists move the date farther back in time with each new discovery, but archaeological sites in the Southwest have been dated to 20,000 years. The mysterious early inhabitants of the Colorado River region were hunters who stalked their Pleistocene prey—including prehistoric horses, camels, mammoths, and mastodons—with stone-tipped spears. By 7,000 B.C., the great Ice Age mammals began to disappear from the New World, and those living in the Southwest developed the Desert Culture. The indigenous people of this new era continued to hunt, but their quarry was smaller—deer, rabbits, lizards, snakes, desert birds, and rodents. They gathered wild plants and seeds for food, including piñon nuts, the fruit of the yucca plant, various berries, and mesquite beans. Around 2,500 B.C., the Native Americans of the region began cultivating maize, or corn. The corn plants were primitive and small, the corn growing in pods. In time, new varieties of corn were introduced into the Southwest. Brought to the region from pre-Columbian Mexico, the new plants were heartier and larger, and the corn harvested from these plants became the staple of the southwestern diet and a mainstay of the people who lived throughout the Colorado River region. Other new plants, such as squash and several varieties of beans, were also cultivated. These three crops—corn, beans, and squash—formed a triad of agricultural products known as the "Three Sisters." Despite an increased reliance on these foods in their diets, the agricultural practices of the inhabitants of the region were rather primitive. Having no plows, Native American farmers used "simple drilling sticks, boring individual holes in the ground and dropping in the seeds."[3]

As southwestern agriculture developed, the Native Americans of the region began erecting more permanent villages, including homes designed for long-term occupation. Earlier residents of the arid regions of the Colorado River Basin had lived in caves, along cliff sides, and in temporary, brush homes, but by 500 B.C., their descendents were building pit houses. Typically circular in design, their foundations were dug a foot or two into the ground and covered with a roof of log beams, a brush framework, and dirt. They included fire pits for cooking and warmth as well as sleeping space and storage pits for food and other accumulated goods. By A.D. 100, pottery had become a utilitarian art form in the Southwest. A new culture, which anthropologists call the Mogollon Culture, had developed.

The Mogollon (the name is derived from a low range of mountains on the southern border between Arizona and New Mexico) became the first people of the Colorado River Basin lands to practice systematic agriculture, erect permanent log and earthen homes, and produce pottery. This culture was situated in the southern half of New Mexico and southeastern Arizona as well as the modern-day Mexican states of Chihuahua and Sonora. The Mogollon farmed the Three Sisters as well as ceremonial tobacco and cotton. The men hunted small game and the women collected wild varieties of plants for food. By A.D. 500, the Mogollon had developed new styles of pottery and basketry, and the bow and arrow came into general use throughout the region. Mogollon pottery included cooking pots, storage containers, and decorative items, sometimes decorated with a fine-lined black-on-white or black-on-red design. During this era, the Native Americans of the Southwest increased their geographical range farther west to include the area along the Little Colorado River, placing them in close proximity to the Grand Canyon.

The Mogollon built the sunken, circular homes their predecessors had erected, and they also created a new form of desert architecture—aboveground housing complexes known today as pueblos. (It was the Spanish who arrived in the region in the 1500s that first used the word *pueblo,* meaning "village," to describe the Mogollon houses.) By 1100, Mogollon villages included as many as 20 or 30 pueblos.

As cotton became an agricultural product of great importance, Mogollon women became noted for their weaving skill; they used looms to create intricate blanket patterns and decorative and colorful clothing that sported feathers and animal furs. One of the most extensive Mogollon cultures developed in the Chaco district of northwestern New Mexico and northern Arizona. Lasting for several hundred years, nearly until the arrival of Europeans into the Southwest, this period of cultural development witnessed an increase in vast, communal pueblo complexes, some rising to five stories in height. Such apartment complexes were home to hundreds of occupants.

Even as the sedentary culture of the Mogollon appeared to hit its peak in the Southwest, climatic changes would soon alter the lives of many Native Americans in the region. By the 1200s, great drought patterns developed, making survival in the harsh environs of the desert lands more difficult, especially for large numbers of people concentrated in village complexes. Some of the inhabitants of these villages began to migrate toward more reliable water sources. Ancestors of the Southern Paiute traveled north to the vicinity of the Grand Canyon and the Colorado River. At nearly the same historical moment, the Pueblo Indians settled along the waters of the Little Colorado and Rio Grande rivers or near various springs throughout the region. The native peoples were still living at these sites when

The Southern Paiute Indians settled the Colorado Plateau of southwestern Utah during the 1100–1200s. The Southern Paiutes were hunter-gatherers but also practiced flood-plain gardening in the Colorado Plateau region.

Spaniards reached them during Coronado's march through the Southwest in 1540.

Between 700 and 1150, a central Arizona culture known as the Cohonina developed in west-central Arizona and spread as far as the south rim of the Grand Canyon. The Cohonina refined the pueblo culture and built pit houses and masonry pueblos. They farmed extensively. About 1150, the Cohonina culture faded, only to be replaced geographically by the Cerbat culture. The Cerbat peoples are the predecessors of the modern-day Walapai and Havasupai Indians. The Cerbat came out of the desert lands along the lower Colorado River Valley into the tablelands of the

Cohonina. Although these people practiced only crude pottery techniques and lived in brush huts or under rock shelters, they survived for hundreds of years. When the Franciscan priest Father Garces reached the region in 1776, it was latter-day Cerbat peoples he encountered.

One of the most important twelfth century pueblo sites was situated on the plateau near the Grand Canyon. Archaeologists have discovered a significant site that included

> . . . 44 small masonry pueblo ruins and . . . 77 agricultural dams. Here, for perhaps a hundred years, a number of family groups . . . planted crops, hunted, and gathered wild plants in the Canyon below. On the Canyon walls nearby are remnants of precipitous trails, marked in one instance by a small masonry storeroom tucked into a recess in the cliff some two thousand feet below the rim; below that, only a few hundred feet above the Colorado River, is a prehistoric wooden bridge that spanned a crevice on a narrow ledge. From this trail it was possible to cross the river and climb out the other side.[4]

As the desert began to experience significant drought patterns between 1150 and 1300, the Southwest saw the development of another significant culture group—the Hohokam. The name was given to these people by the Pima tribe centuries later. The Pima referred to these ancient residents of south-central Arizona, who had left village sites as well as other evidence of their previous existence behind, as *hohokam* or "the vanished ones."

The Hohokam lived along various tributaries of the Colorado River, including the San Pedro, Salt, and Gila rivers. They were successful agriculturists, lived in subterranean homes, and worked pottery, just as the Mogollon had done. In their southern Arizona homelands, the Hohokam could not rely on adequate game or even wild plants to provide their main food sources. Therefore, they developed extensive farming systems that relied heavily on irrigation.

The Hohokam may have become the expert irrigation engineers of the entire Southwest. They built canals and ditches that

THE HAVASUPAI, THEN AND NOW

Some early Native American groups no longer call the Colorado River Basin home (some do not even exist today), but others continue to dwell in the region even after nearly a millennium. Two of those Indian groups are the Havasupai and the Hualapai.

Since at least A.D. 1100, the Havasupai have called Cataract Canyon in the Grand Canyon their home. Despite their long-term presence in the canyon, their numbers have never been very extensive. As late as the seventeenth century, approximately 250 Havasupai lived in Cataract Canyon. Today, only 400 or so remain. That number is down from the 1970s, when more than 600 lived in the small side canyon where Havasu Creek "spills down a series of enchanting waterfalls and, like the Little Colorado, blends its blue waters with the main stream of the Grand Canyon."* Descended from the early Cohonina, the Havasupai are also known as the "People of the Blue Green Water."

The early ancestors of the Havasupai gathered desert plants from the Colorado River at the 1,800-foot elevation and hunted on the slopes of the San Francisco Peaks, which tower at 12,000 feet. It is likely that the early People of the Blue Green Water may never have been disturbed by the various Spanish groups that reached the Grand Canyon during the seventeenth and eighteenth centuries. This allowed them to continue their centuries-old lifestyle, adapting only to changes that came to them second-hand, usually through trading with the Hopi, who introduced them to European cloth goods, fruit trees, and the horse.

diverted water to their crop fields. They also constructed dams along rivers, using finely woven grass mats as sluice gates that could be opened and closed to divert water where it was needed most. The irrigation systems of the Hohokam were so extensive that some of their water canals ran ten miles in length. The Hohokam built between 200 and 250 miles of canals along two of the Colorado's tributaries, the Salt and Gila rivers.

For nearly 1,500 years, the Hohokam people developed their unique culture. Through most of that time (from A.D. 1 to 1,500) the center of Hohokam culture was a village called Snaketown,

By the late 1800s, the American government created a Havasupai reservation in the canyon, limiting the canyon people to just over 500 acres and denying them access to their traditional upland hunting and gathering lands. To make up for the loss, the Havasupai took up farming and became known for their peach cultivation. They also began raising cattle.

Several severe epidemics in the early twentieth century reduced the Havasupai population to 100. The traditional tribal power of the group declined dramatically. As late as the 1950s, the Havasupai were suffering from a lack of economic opportunity and significant cultural losses. By 1975, extensive lobbying efforts persuaded the U.S. government to cede 185,000 acres of canyon land back to the Havasupai, a piece of land 350 times larger than their 518 acres. Much of that land is now used by the Havasupai for cattle grazing.

Today, the Havasupai people still live in the canyon lands of their ancestors. They have direct contact with tourists who visit the Grand Canyon's Hualapai Trail, where the Indians maintain a campground and a modern lodge. Two hundred years ago, their ancestors adopted the horse into the Havasupai culture; today, many of the tribe members still travel on horseback. No paved road into the canyon of the Havasupai exists.

* Quoted in Barry M. Pritzker, *A Native American Encyclopedia: History, Culture, and Peoples* (New York: Oxford University Press, 2000), 30.

located south of modern-day Phoenix. Snaketown boasted more than 100 underground pit houses situated on 300 acres. The Hohokam culture was more advanced than that of the Mogollon, and Hohokam peoples worked with textiles, clay, metallurgy, and stone. Their pottery, commonly red-on-buff, included utilitarian items and decorative pieces, among them clay human figurines. They hammered out copper items and made mirrors from iron pyrites. Evidence suggests that the Hohokam had extensive trade connections with the more advanced peoples to the south, including the Aztecs of Mexico.

Archaeological excavations at their village sites have unearthed "skeletons of macaws, colorful birds indigenous to South and Central America [which] the Hohokam kept . . . as pets."[5]

Contemporaries of the Hohokam, centering their culture in yet another region of the Colorado River Basin, were the Anasazi. Their name, meaning "ancient ones," was given to them by the modern Navajo. The Anasazi culture began to come into its own around 100 B.C., and its progenitors lived along the desert plateau known today as the "Four Corners"—the area where the states of Arizona, Colorado, Utah, and New Mexico meet. Adapting their culture through several anthropological stages, the Anasazi were living in pueblos by A.D. 750.

One of the most important and mysterious of the Anasazi pueblo complexes is known today as Pueblo Bonito and is located in Chaco Canyon in northwestern New Mexico. Its ruins reveal that as many as 1,000 people at a time lived in the complex, a great D-shaped system of pueblos that rose to a height of five stories and included 800 rooms. Beyond the large semicircle of houses, storage buildings, social centers, and plazas, Pueblo Bonito also had elaborate, sunken rooms, lined with stone and covered over with flat roofs of beams, brush, and mud. These were great ceremonial centers known as *kivas*.

For their time, the Anasazi were quite advanced. Their social order included well-defined roles and tasks for builders, weavers, agriculturists, potters, and other craftsmen. Their artwork was exquisite and included "turquoise jewelry, mosaics and brilliantly dyed textiles of cotton and feathers."[6] Just as other southwestern civilizations of Native Americans were forced to abandon their village sites when the weather centered on a drought cycle, however, the Anasazi were abandoning their villages by the 1200s. (Anthropologists point to a drought for the years 1276–1299, which helped destroy Anasazi culture). They migrated to other, more hospitable locales, including lands along major rivers, such as the Colorado and Rio Grande.

After the Anasazi moved from their great pueblos, they developed into more modern native groups. Between 1300 and

1550, the Anasazi became known as Pueblo Indians. They continued to live in pueblos, at sites such as Verde Valley, the Tonto basin, and along the banks of the Upper Salt River. When the Spanish reached the region in the 1540s, they found the Pueblos living in 80 or so scattered villages and numbering about 16,000 people. Their descendents include the Hopi and Zuni peoples, who still call the American Southwest and the Colorado River Basin their home.

2

New People
Reach the Colorado

V arious groups of Native Americans had occupied the Colorado River valley and its surrounding regions for thousands of years, their lives changing little from one generation to the next. They continued century after century, living in well-delineated social systems and relying on hunting, gathering, and limited agriculture to sustain their desert-land cultures. By the sixteenth century, life for countless Native Americans in the Western Hemisphere, including those living in Colorado, was about to change—more dramatically than it had in four millennia. The catalyst for this extraordinary change in the lives of Native Americans and in the future of the Colorado River was the arrival of the first white men to North America.

After the initial voyages of the great Genoese explorer and seaman Christopher Columbus in the 1490s, his sponsoring nation, the kingdom of Spain, soon dispatched hundreds, then thousands of soldiers, bureaucrats, churchmen, and adventurers to the New World to establish Spanish rule over Native American lands. Within a generation, the Spanish *conquistador* (meaning "conqueror") Hernando Cortés reached the extensive empire of the Aztec people in modern-day Mexico and conquered them. The Aztec kingdom had been built on vast quantities of silver and gold extracted from numberless mines, a fact discovered by the Spanish as they defeated native empires in both Central and South America. These precious metals became of the basis of Spain's New World economy and made Spain eager to pursue additional discoveries of such riches.

Hearing rumors of rich cities of gold to the north, the Spanish soon took an interest in the unexplored lands. In search of treasure, they sent conquistadors into modern-day California and the American Southwest, including the Colorado River Basin region. In 1540, Cortés' successor, a Spanish viceroy named Mendoza, dispatched a fellow conquistador, Francisco Vasquez de Coronado, in search of a mysterious land called Cíbola, a complex of seven golden cities. Rumors related by local natives included stories about the fabled emperor of the "Gran Quivera" who slept beneath a tree, lulled to rest by the endless tinkling of thousands of small, golden bells tied to its branches. There was also the story of the leader of El Dorado, known as the "Gilded Man," whose body was oiled each morning, then coated with gold dust. Every night, the Gilded Man washed the gold dust off in a local lake. After many years the shores of the lake had become laden with golden sand. Another story told of a land of women ruled by a Queen Califa, whose kingdom contained an endless quantity of gold and pearls. Such stories intrigued many Spaniards and prompted some of them to find out for themselves whether or not they were true.

In the spring of 1536, Spanish strangers arrived on foot in the Mexican capital of Tenochtitlán, the former center of Aztec power. Alvaro Nuñez Cabeza de Vaca, the leader of this group, told a fantastic story of having been shipwrecked eight years earlier off the coast of either modern-day Florida or Texas. He and a handful of his crew wandered for years in the Southwest. Eventually, they reached the sanctuary of the Mexican capital. When Cabeza de Vaca and his men were brought before Cortés, they told their story again and were soon asked about the seven cities of Cíbola. Cortés soon received the assurance he was seeking. According to Cabeza de Vaca, the cities existed; he described them as "gleaming cities containing palaces ornamented with sapphires, rubies and turquoise, gold without end."[7]

Desperate to dispatch explorers into the region in search of the golden cities, Cortés tried to get permission and money for the effort. Financially ruined, he returned to Spain before permission was granted. By 1539, however, his successor, the new viceroy, Don Antonio de Mendoza, had received orders from the Spanish monarch to send a small fleet of ships to Mexico's northern Pacific Coast. The fleet's captain, Francisco de Ulloa, left Acapulco on July 8, sailing north in the Sea of Cortez. At that time, the Spanish believed that modern-day California was an island and that this body of water separated it from the mainland. As his three ships sailed farther north, Ulloa became curious about the waters in which he was sailing. In his journal, he recorded, "[We] always found more shallow water, and the sea thick, and very muddy . . . whereupon we rode all night in five fathom water, and we perceived the sea to run with so great a rage into the land that it was a thing much to be marveled at."[8]

The following morning, Ulloa and his crew became convinced they were not floating in a sea at all, but a long, narrow gulf, fed by water from inland, perhaps from lakes. Ulloa wrote, "There were divers opinions amongst us, and some thought that that current entered into these lakes, and also that some great river might be the cause thereof."[9] From their shipboard vantage point, Ulloa and his men may have been the first Europeans to observe the waters of the mouth of the Colorado River.

Ulloa turned his ships around, perhaps frightened that they might founder if he proceeded farther. He ordered one vessel to return to Mexico City while he sailed south around the Baja Peninsula and up the Pacific Coast of California. No one ever heard from him again.

The Spanish dream of Cíbola did not die with Ulloa's disappearance from Californian waters. Mendoza had already sent another party of explorers into the unknown of the Colorado River region. The group of explorers included a Franciscan monk named Marcos de Niza and a black slave named Esteban, who had previously accompanied Cabeza de Vaca through the region. During their travels, Esteban went ahead of the priest, gaining the acceptance of the Native Americans he encountered by declaring himself to be a god. He was tall and well built, and the locals generally accepted his claim. When Esteban reached the Zuni pueblo of Hawikah in southern Arizona, he sent word back to the Franciscan father, telling him that he had found one of the seven cities of gold. Unfortunately, Esteban was soon killed by some natives who did not accept his story of being a deity.

In due time, Father Marcos reached the Zuni town, a pueblo community perched atop a mesa. He described what he saw as "gilded by the summer sun, shimmering impressively in the bleak and angular land."[10] Certain that he had discovered one of the cities of gold, Marcos reported back to Mendoza, telling him that the legends were, in fact, true.

Mendoza responded quickly to the news and began raising a new expedition that would move in two directions simultaneously. One group was to travel in the path of Father Marcos while the other was to sail by sea in search of Ulloa. Both groups were to stay in communication with one another. Leading the land expedition was a conquistador who was also governor of a northern Mexican province, 30-year-old Francisco Vásquez de Coronado. Coronado set out from New Spain in February of 1540, with 300 soldiers "in burnished armor riding horses whose ornate trappings hung to the ground,"[11] followed by a large number of servants, priests, and native warriors.

Coronado and his men arrived in the Southwest by ship, landing at the Spanish seaport of San Miguel de Culiacán. From there, they set out overland toward the Colorado River region. Three months later, Captain Hernando de Alarcon also reached Culiacán, just missing the departure of Coronado and his expeditionary forces. Adding Coronado's ship, the *San Gabriel,* to his own fleet of two vessels, Alarcon continued sailing north, looking for any sign of Coronado. By late August, he reached the same head of the gulf that Ulloa had reached, and dangerous summer tides drove all of his ships onto sandbars. Many of Alarcon's crew wanted to abandon the treacherous waters, but Alarcon pushed on, driven by Mendoza's orders. Alarcon wrote:

> I resolved that although I had known I should have lost the ships, I would not have ceased for anything to have seen the head [of the gulf]. . . . And we passed forward with much ado . . . to seek and find the channel. And it pleased God that. . . we came to the very bottom of the bay, where we found a very mighty river, which ran with so great fury of a storm, that we could hardly sail against it.[12]

Pressing on, with the help of local natives who were willing to tow the boarding boats on Alarcon's ships, the Spanish captain and his crew sailed up the difficult waters of the Colorado to the mouth of the Gila River. Here, Alarcon met with natives that knew of Esteban, who had been killed by the Hawikah

The Kuaua Pueblo was inhabited by Pueblo Indians from 1300 until 1590. Spanish explorer Francisco Vasquez de Coronado visited the area, which is just north of present-day Albuquerque, New Mexico, in 1540, during his search for the seven golden cities.

pueblo people. Failing to connect with any of Coronado's party, Alarcon's men buried some supplies for the land party and then sailed back downriver to the mouth of the Colorado. The Spaniards had reached the river, refusing to turn back as Ulloa and his men had done. After three months of exploring the Colorado, they departed, but not before taking time to name the violent river they had struggled against for many weeks. The name they bestowed on the river was El Rio de Buena Guia (the River of Good Guidance).

As Alarcon struggled against the turbulent waters of the Colorado, Coronado's land party reached the pueblo town of Hawikah, home to a band of Zuni Indians. Much to Coronado's disappointment, the town was not filled with great golden riches. After subduing the Zuni at Hawikah, the Spanish exploration party set out in search of other settlements, always keeping the tales of Cíbola at the center of their mission. During the fall of 1540, Coronado sent out search parties of soldiers who fanned out across the bleak countryside of the Southwest. One party of two dozen or so, led by Melchior Diaz, was sent west in search of Alarcon. The men followed a well-worn Indian trail, El Camino del Diablo (the Road of the Devil). After traveling more than 400 miles across the barren brushlands of Arizona, Diaz finally reached the Colorado River. He named it the Rio de Tizon (the Firebrand River), after local natives who carried torches to ward off mosquitoes. He was, of course, unaware that Alarcon had already christened the river by another Spanish name. In fact, Diaz had unwittingly crossed the path of Alarcon and had discovered the following inscription on a tree: "Alarcon reached this point; there are letters at the foot of this tree." Continuing their journey, the Spaniards under Diaz crossed the Colorado River on rafts built for them by the local natives. They soon reached

> . . . sand banks of hot ashes which it was impossible to cross without being drowned as in a sea. The ground . . . trembled like a sheet of paper, so that it seemed as if there were lakes under them. It seemed wonderful and like something infernal, for the ashes to bubble up here in several places.[13]

Diaz and his party had stumbled onto Mullet Island in the Salton Sink (which was later covered with the waters of Volcano Lake when the river shifted channels in 1910). Whether aware of his achievement or not, Diaz had become the first European to reach California by land. Turning around, he headed back to the east. Diaz met with an untimely death when he became impaled on the "butt of his own lance while attempting to spear a rabbit."[14]

Another of Coronado's search parties also reached the banks of the Colorado River, but at a more spectacular location. A Spanish captain, Garcia Lopez de Cardenas, and the 25 Spaniards under his command, first sighted the river from the edge of the Grand Canyon, making them the first documented Europeans to see the now-famous gorge. One of Coronado's scribes, Castaneda, later wrote of Cardenas's discovery:

> After they had gone 20 days, they came to the banks of the river. It seemed to be more than three or four leagues in an air line across to the other bank of the stream that flowed between them. The country was elevated and full of low, twisted pines, very cold, and lying open to the north. . . . They spent three days on this bank, looking for a passage down to the river, which looked from above as if the water was six feet across, although the Indians said it was half a league wide. It was impossible to descend [although] the three lightest and agile men made an attempt to go down . . . and went down until those who were above were unable to keep sight of them.[15]

After six months of exploration, Coronado had had enough of the Southwest and the region of the Colorado River. He had failed to find the location of the elusive Seven Cities of Cíbola. All he had reached were the mud huts of the Zuni. Although his men had succeeded in discovering the Colorado River, had beheld the magnificence of the Grand Canyon, and had explored the region's immense tract of desert lands, they had found no gold. The Spanish conquistador remained in the area through-out the winter, taking up quarters at a site near present-day Albuquerque, New Mexico. The following spring, he continued his pursuit of gold, traveling as far as the eastern portion of modern-day Kansas. After thousands of fruitless miles, he returned empty handed to the Valley of Mexico in 1542, "without honor—without illusions."[16]

Despite an expedition that had determined that California was not an island and had led to the discovery of some of the

THE GRAND CANYON

When Spanish explorers reached the rims of the Grand Canyon, the most magnificent geologic feature of North America, they saw no value in the exotic landscape. For them, the canyon merely impeded movement from one bank of the Colorado River to the other.

Today, however, the Grand Canyon, named by nineteenth-century American explorer John Wesley Powell, attracts millions of visitors, people drawn by the raw, geologic beauty of the red-rock chasm. The canyon is 277 miles long, runs more than a mile deep in many places, and yawns as wide as 18 miles across. Grand Canyon National Park measures 1,900 square miles and includes 1.2 million acres. The canyon is an ancient giant. Geologists date its oldest rocks at 1.7 billion years.

The canyon's unique geology was formed largely through erosion caused by the Colorado River. Additional erosion was caused by wind, rain, and melting snow. Today, the Colorado drops 2,215 feet within the park boundaries of the Grand Canyon. Through all this erosion, the canyon has become an endless theater of sheer rock walls, multihued rock formations, and natural shapes formed out of granite, limestone, sandstone, and shale, which change their appearance and color as the sun moves across the desert sky. At sunset, the canyon is at its most vivid, its red and brown layered walls brilliant with reflections of filtered light. Elevations within Grand Canyon vary greatly from 1,250 to more than 9,000 feet. The canyon's popular South Rim stands 7,400 feet above sea level.

Not only is the Grand Canyon a geological wonder, it is also a natural haven for desert wildlife and plant types. Approximately 275 species of birds can be found in Grand Canyon National Park. The park is also home to 120 other animal types, including 67 animal species, such as bighorn sheep, elk, mountain lions, mule deer, antelope, and more exotic creatures, such as white-tailed Kaibab squirrels and pink Grand Canyon rattlesnakes, which are found nowhere else on earth. The waters of the Colorado within park boundaries teem with 16 species of fish. Forty-six species of reptiles and amphibians also call the Grand Canyon home. A vast array of plant life, 1,500 species, further beautifies the canyon. Among these plant varieties are the cliff rose, fernbush, mountain mahogany, prickly pear cactus, and cholla.

Although most of the 2.5 million people who view the wonders of the great canyon are tourists, the canyon has been home to humans for thousands of years and thus attracts those interested in science and culture. Anthropologists have discovered at least 2,000 Anasazi Indian sites within the national park's boundaries. Even today, hundreds of Havasupai Indians live in the canyon, on a reservation in a side gorge called Havasu Canyon.

greatest natural resources of the Southwest, the Spanish wasted little time on further explorations into the region of the Colorado, convinced it held no value for them. For the remainder of the sixteenth century, the Colorado River—known by Spaniards as Rio de Tizon or El Rio de Buena Guia—continued to flow into the Gulf of California, ignored and nearly forgotten.

3

The Colorado Rediscovered

Throughout the 1500s, the Spanish monarchy extended its power throughout the Americas until its New World empire stretched from California to South America. The lands Spain claimed were so numerous, so far flung, that its administrators and conquistadors were able to concentrate only on those regions that yielded the greatest reward. Lands abundant in great wealth, especially gold and silver, became centers of commerce, development, governmental power, and slavery. The region watered by the Colorado River remained a wilderness, a wasteland that had no observable value. It might be a land where poor Native Americans could scratch out a living, but it could never offer significant opportunities for exploitation by one of the most powerful kingdoms in all of Europe. Once Coronado returned from the Southwest without discovering great wealth, the region remained much as it had been for countless centuries.

By the 1600s, however, after much of the wealth of gold and silver had been tapped from New World mines, attempts were made to further the extent of Spanish power in every remote corner of the Americas, including the region of the Colorado River. One aspect of Spanish expansion was the arrival of those who looked not so much at the land and the natural resources that might be turned into a profit for the Spanish crown but at the people of the region. They were not government officials, soldiers, or otherwise greedy men ready to take for themselves and their king. They were priests.

From 1604 until the late 1770s, the Colorado River region, as well as the Southwest as a whole, felt the impact of the work of Jesuit and then Franciscan priests. Both were priestly orders of the Catholic Church, and they entered the region intent on spreading the word of God and converting Native Americans from their natural religions to a belief in Jesus Christ.

One of the first priests to arrive in the Colorado River region was Father Francisco de Escobar. In October of 1604, the first governor of New Mexico, Juan de Onate, set out from San Gabriel de los Españoles, his outpost capital situated on the banks of the Rio Grande River Valley of northern New Mexico.

With 30 soldiers and two priests, he headed west toward the Pacific Ocean. For several years, Onate had dreamed of developing an access road from the California coast to New Mexico to encourage further colonization in his underpopulated province. (Onate had gained a terrible reputation in the region for his harshness toward the local natives, whom he had violently subdued just a few years earlier. It was a struggle that had ended in the slaughter of 800 men, women, and children.)

As the Spaniards marched across New Mexico, they reached a settlement of Hopi Indians. Just beyond their villages, Onate reached a river thick with red mud. He named the stream *Colorado* meaning "reddish color." The river that he had reached, however, was not the true Colorado but the river known today as the Little Colorado, which runs diagonally from southeast to northwest across modern-day Arizona.

The party descended to the headwaters of the Verde River. Then, led by local Indians who wore small crosses they had probably received from Alarcon decades earlier, the Spaniards followed Bill Williams Fork (which they called the San Andreas) to its juncture with the Colorado River. In his journal, Father Escobar reveals that the men christened the Colorado with yet a third Spanish name, calling it the Rio de Buena Esperanza (River of Good Hope). Escobar wrote:

> Where it joins the San Andreas it flows from northwest to southeast, and from here turns northeast-southwest to the sea or Gulf of California, bearing on either side high ranges, between which it forms a very wide river bottom, all densely populated by people on both sides of the river, clear to the sea.[17]

Of course, the people Father Escobar referred to were not fellow Spaniards but Native Americans whose ancestors had lived along the Colorado River for centuries. Escobar estimated the indigenous population along the river at 30,000. For three months, Onate's party followed the river and Escobar spent "many days . . . investigating and converting heathens into minions [followers] of the Lord."[18]

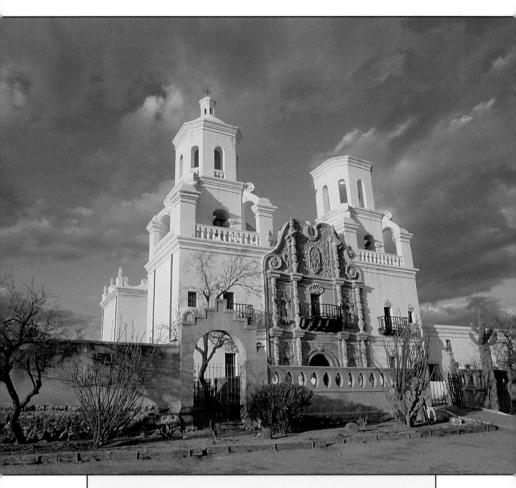

The Jesuits, a priestly order of the Catholic Church, founded the church of the Mission San Xavier del Bac south of Tucson, Arizona, in the late seventeenth century. Both the Jesuits and Franciscans spread the word of God to the Native Americans of the Colorado River region.

By January of 1605, the Spanish soldiers and priests reached the mouth of the Colorado River, and Escobar noted, "we arrived with great joy at the sea or Gulf of California."[19] Discovering that his dream of riches in the pearl trade was not to be, Onate led his men back to New Mexico, following El Camino del Diablo.

Along the way, they passed the Zuni pueblos. There, on the walls of a sandstone cliff, Onate ordered an inscription to be carved, marking his passing through the region:

> PASSED BY HERE THE COMMANDER
> DON JUAN DE ONATE FROM THE
> DISCOVERY OF THE SOUTH SEA
> ON THE 16TH OF APRIL, YEAR 1605

Although Onate had not actually discovered the South Sea (the Spanish name for the Pacific Ocean) and had not succeeded in establishing any economic extension of his New Mexican province, Father Escobar had managed to further the cause of Christianity, at least for the moment. Onate and his men had also managed to establish a road over 3,000 miles of hostile desert country in less than one year, but the trail was little traveled. Not until 1621 did another Spanish party, which included 47 soldiers and another priest, Father Jimenez, try to replicate the journey of the Onate expedition. They progressed as far as the lands west of the Hopi pueblos but turned back, defeated by the rough terrain and rugged canyons. Then, several local native communities, including those of the Hopi and Pueblos, rebelled against the Spaniards on their lands. Before the uprisings ended, the Indians killed more than 400 Spanish residents in New Mexico, including 21 priests. According to Hopi stories, the Spanish fathers' deaths "atoned for the gift of Hopi girls given by the priests to Spanish soldiers."[20] So extensive was the Indian rebellion in the Colorado River region that the Spanish largely abandoned the province. For most of the century to follow, "the Colorado would not again be encountered by civilized man."[21]

The next priest to make his way into the Colorado region was not a Spaniard but a "transplanted Austrian"[22] who arrived in New Spain in 1681. The priest, Father Eusebio Francisco Kino, first established a mission amid the bleakness of Baja California, but it proved unsuccessful. The Church then sent the stalwart Jesuit into an even more remote region—the lands of the

Colorado—where he was to minister to the Pima Indians. Here he made his home for a quarter of a century, spreading the Gospel along the rivers of the Southwest, including tributaries of the Colorado.

Kino seemed to thrive in the desolate region; "he crossed and recrossed its desert and mountain wastes many times during his twenty-four years."[23] He established outposts throughout the region, including San Dionysio at the confluence of the Gila and Colorado Rivers. In 1601, after having a vision, he became intent on establishing a road to California. (Sixty years had passed since Onate established his route to southern California, but the trail had not been maintained.) That November, Kino set out with a handful of Native Americans as his servants and traveling companions. They reached the Colorado and followed it to the southwest. He picked up more Indian companions as he traveled the river. While on the Colorado, the wandering priest named the river, as other earlier European arrivals had done. This time, the river was christened Rio de los Martires (River of the Martyrs). Finally, Kino forded the river at Old Colonia Lerdo, becoming the first European since Melchior Diaz to cross the Colorado. To aid in his crossing, the Indians built a raft and placed Kino in a basket: "I seated myself in it and crossed very comfortably and pleasantly, without the least risk."[24] When he reached the mouth of the river, he was the first European in a century to do so.

As Father Kino traveled throughout the region of Sonora, across modern-day Arizona, he met with hundreds of Native Americans, visiting their villages and enjoying their company and friendship. Throughout his journey, he took care to create as accurate a map as he could under difficult circumstances. No accurate maps of the New Mexican landscape existed at the time, and Kino's contribution was extraordinary. His work as a Catholic priest made him a legend among the indigenous peoples of the Colorado River Basin and his map brought him additional fame. For many decades to follow, Kino's map went unchallenged in its accuracy. On this map, Kino decided to rename the great southwestern river that had already been named several times by various Spanish explorers and church-men since the 1500s (and by Kino himself as Rio de los Martires). He called it Colorado. Thus, the red, muddy river was first given its permanent name.

Kino died in 1711, and few Jesuits or other Spaniards followed in his immediate footsteps. More than 30 years passed before Padre Jacobo Sedelmair, who floated down the Gila River and reached the banks of the Colorado in 1744, arrived in the region. In 1761, another priest, a Jesuit named Alonso de Posadas, reached the Green River, another tributary of the Colorado. Each of these Jesuit missionaries accomplished a mission for the Catholic Church in doing their work with the local natives, and they were also crucial in "opening up much unknown country in the New World,"[25] including the Colorado region.

The day of the Jesuits—or the Black Robes as they were called by the local natives—was over by 1767. In that year, the king ordered all Jesuits out of New Spain, and they were replaced by a new order of missionaries—the Franciscans. By the 1770s, Franciscans—known as the Gray Robes—reached the Southwest region. One of the first was Father Francisco Garces. Father Garces entered the Colorado River region as part of an expedition organized to establish a road from northern Sonora to the San Fernando Valley in southern California. In January, nearly three dozen men, along with 140 horses and 65 head of cattle, set out along the existing trail from the confluence of the Gila and Colorado rivers. They marked out the road further as they progressed, reaching California after two months. A second expedition followed, this one with plans to extend a road to modern-day San Francisco Bay. Father Garces was among the 235 people involved in this 1775 mission, but he abandoned the group completely at the mouth of the Gila River, intent on exploring on his own and on seeking out "the disposition of the natives toward the Christians."[26]

Throughout the first six months of 1776, Garces crossed the Mojave Desert, traveled down the Mojave River, crossed the Colorado River, walked the Colorado Plateau, and reached the Grand Canyon. He was, in fact, the first European to view the Grand Canyon from the western side, possibly near El Tovar. While at the canyon, Father Garces climbed down into one of its side canyons to Cataract Creek and discovered the Havasupai, a small Indian tribe. During his descent, the trail proved too steep for his mule, forcing the priest to use a ladder on portions of the canyon walls. He had little success converting the Havasupai, who lived on 400 acres of the canyon bottom, to Christianity. While in the canyon, Garces marveled at what he saw, taking note of "the sight of the most profound canyons that ever onward continue, and within these flows the Rio Colorado." No other European had visited the canyon since Coronado's men arrived in 1540. Having no success in converting the canyon's residents, Father Garces returned to his mission base of San Xavier in southern Arizona, arriving there in September of 1776.

Over the years that followed, Garces was instrumental in helping establish missions throughout the Colorado region. He made five trips through the Colorado River region, logged 5,000 miles, and ministered to 25,000 Indians from nine different tribes. The missions he established were often protected by local garrisons of Spanish soldiers. Unfortunately, in 1781, after some soldiers let their horses into the bean fields of the Yuma Indians, the natives attacked the Spanish outpost, killing all the Spanish residents, including Father Garces. The attackers were led by a Yuma known as "Captain Palma." Years earlier, Palma had been converted to Christianity—by Father Garces.

Father Garces had worked to establish a road through the Colorado region. Another priest, Father Francisco Silvestre Velez de Escalante, was involved in a similar endeavor. Escalante was interested in establishing a northern land route to California. During the summer of 1776, Escalante, along with another priest and several soldiers, marched northwest out of Santa Fe. They crossed the San Juan River along the border between modern-day Colorado and New Mexico, then cut southwest beyond Durango until they crossed the Colorado River just to the west of Grand Junction. In a long-ranging arc, the priests and soldiers walked into Utah and reached the Green River just below the southern border of Wyoming.

By September, the party had reached the Wasatch Range and the valley of Utah Lake. They were not certain where they were, and their food supply and their morale were low. In early October, the weary group faced another problem as snow began to fall. Knowing that staying where they were was inviting disaster, they had to decide whether to move forward or go back. On October 8, the men agreed to cast lots to determine whether they should continue to California or return to the Colorado and then to Santa Fe. Father Escalante described the scene. "Concluding our prayers, we cast lots and it came out in favor of Cosnina [the Colorado]. We all accepted this, thanks be to God, willingly and joyfully."[27] They wandered for weeks, looking for the Colorado River. Their food ran out and they subsisted on piñon nuts, roots, and roasted cactus. Early in November they stumbled on the Colorado and crossed just north of Marble Canyon, using "ropes . . . down to the vicinity of the ford."[28] The men had to carve steps in the cliff side for their horses. In this manner, Escalante and his party became the first Europeans to cross the Grand Canyon. They reached Santa Fe three months later

For most of two centuries, Jesuit and Franciscan priests had helped explore, map, and traverse the Colorado River Basin. They participated in important expeditions, designed to further the extent of Spanish power and the influence of the Catholic Church in the region. Many were men of sacrifice, giving decades of their lives in service to the faith. The Native Americans of the Colorado River Basin sometimes aided these priests and sometimes killed them. Some heeded their spiritual message and became followers of Jesus Christ. Whether the priests succeeded in their missions or failed, they all remained enchanted with the landscape, lured by the grandeur of its canyon lands and painted deserts. They crossed the waters of the Colorado, the Gila, the Green, the San Juan, and other rivers in the region. They were the first Europeans to cross the Colorado River upriver from the Grand Canyon and the first to walk across the wild, forbidding mesas of the Great Basin. Even today, the legacy of their faith continues in the Southwest: Mission churches still dot the barren landscapes of Arizona, New Mexico, and California. As representatives of the Spanish Empire in the New World, they were the last of the line. The same year Father Garces viewed the sandstone walls of the Grand Canyon from its western side, the Second Continental Congress, meeting in Philadelphia, signed the Declaration of Independence, giving birth to the United States of America. The power of Spain was already declining by the 1700s, and as the nineteenth century opened, the Colorado River region was poised to receive new visitors, new explorers, and new residents—the Anglo Americans, or former British colonists.

The Americans
Reach the River

As late as the Civil War (1861–1865), much of the Colorado River system remained a mystery to Anglo Americans. Although three centuries had passed since the days of the Spanish discovery of the Grand Canyon by a handful of Coronado's men, the river remained uncharted. Largely unexplored, its value as a resource was yet to be fully appreciated by non-Indians. Several mountain men and fur trappers throughout the first half of the nineteenth century had reached the river and floated, sometimes perilously, down portions of its rugged rapids. Some, such as fur trapper James Ohio Pattie, may have actually reached the rim of the Grand Canyon and viewed the swirling waters of the Colorado.

In 1825, former military officer and fur trapper General William H. Ashley became the first white man of record to float much of the Colorado, a trip he and his men were forced to make after Crow Indians stole most of their horses. Ashley described the difficulties of passing through Flaming Gorge: "We proceeded down the river which is closely confined between two very high mountains. . . . The rocks that fall in the river from the walls of the mountain make the passage in some places dangerous."[29] Yet any and all of the limited explorations made of the Colorado River by the 1860s were fragmented, revealing little about the great western waterway. As one historian has stated, "It still was a riddle, walled in mystery and susceptible to curiously insistent myths—not the least of which was the 'certainty' . . . that the Colorado was the . . . West's natural thoroughfare to the Pacific."[30]

During the late 1820s, a brash, young British naval lieutenant made an attempt to sail his 25-ton schooner *Bruja* into the mouth of the Colorado. Lieutenant R.W.H. Hardy was, in 1826, a 20-year-veteran of the Royal Navy. Dispatched to the Gulf of California to look for valuable pearl beds, Hardy entered the main channel of the Colorado on July 20. After his boat ran aground on a sandbar, the lieutenant set out to explore the unknown river. In doing so, he may have been the first white man ever to reach the Colorado's mouth. Hardy later wrote of his experience: "I was now gazing at a vast extent of country visited only by the elements. It is probably in the same state that it was ages ago, and perhaps I am the first person, from creation up to the present time, whose eyes have ever beheld it."[31]

With the exactitude of a well-trained cartographer, Hardy proceeded to take sounds on the river, chart its channels, and otherwise record his findings along the lower Colorado. He named everything he saw—islands, channels, river branches. After three weeks, his schooner floated off its sandbar and on August 15, the *Bruja* slipped quietly south, its commander having registered all his discoveries. A book on his findings, *Travels in the Interior of Mexico, 1825–28*, was published, but despite the interest aroused by his published account, no one followed up on his adventures for another 25 years.

Then, in 1850, the United States government began to make its mark on the Colorado's long, winding history. That year, a military fort was built at the mouth of the Gila River. To supply the new outpost, a 120-ton transport schooner, the *Invincible,* was sent up the Colorado. The schooner ran into trouble at the same spot where Hardy's *Bruja* had run aground. The army followed up its failed effort with several attempts to dispatch a small steamboat that would draw less water, allowing it to make its way up the shallow waters of the Colorado's mouth. In 1851, a flatboat freighter named George A. Johnson became the first to navigate the Colorado's mouth. Johnson sent a small, stern-wheel steamboat, the *Yuma,* upriver to the army's year-old fort. The underpowered *Yuma* struggled against the silt-laden waters of the river. Throughout the 1850s, Johnson tried to add to his navigating business on the lower Colorado. He put eight steamboats on the river; several sank or exploded. Bad luck and the difficulties of steaming through the thick waters of the great western river finally ended Johnson's efforts as the founder of the Colorado Steam Navigation Company.

One of the most successful explorations of the lower Colorado during the 1850s took place under the auspices of the United States War Department. In 1857, the department ordered the

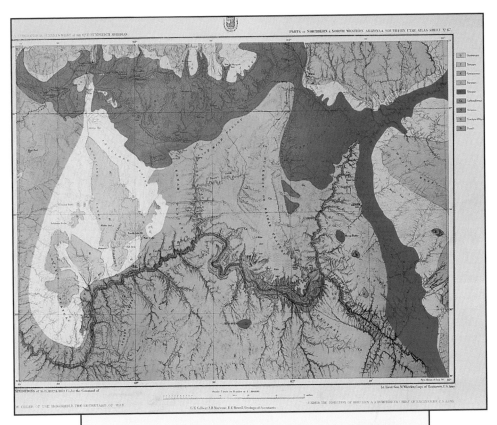

A geological map of the Grand Canyon shown from above. The Colorado River remained largely uncharted until the mid-1800s.

building of a steel-hulled steamer, the *Explorer,* a boat specifically designed for use on the Colorado. Built in Philadelphia, the steamboat was shipped in pieces around South America to San Francisco. Then it was delivered to the mouth of the Colorado where it was rebuilt, a difficult process that took a month to complete. When finally reconstructed, the *Explorer* was dispatched to the waters of the Colorado. Lieutenant Joseph Christmas Ives was ordered to explore the mouth and lower portion of the river. Chugging upriver, Ives reached Fort Yuma on January 5, 1858. Less than a week later, the *Explorer* was readied for further travel upriver. With two dozen men onboard, including an artist and a topographer-engraver to record the sites along the river, Ives set out. After running aground almost immediately, the crew struggled to get the 58-foot-long steamer back into the river's main current, and the voyage of discovery continued. Progress was difficult. The *Explorer* managed to cover only 150 miles of the river in a month, running into constant obstacles, such as "sandbars, disappearing channels, hidden rocks, and the vagaries of the current itself."[32]

On more than one occasion, the Explorer's engine stopped, and the crew was forced to pull the boat upriver with a towrope. On February 9, the steamer reached Mojave Canyon, where Ives met with the Mojave Indians. While encamped with the Mojave, the American party convinced one of the locals to serve as a guide on the next leg of their upriver journey. After two weeks at the canyon, the *Explorer* again chugged up the Colorado. Over the next month, Ives and his crew perilously navigated their heavy steamer through difficult waters and dangerous rapids. Writing in his journal, Ives described the difficulties he and his men encountered as they pushed up the Colorado:

> The twenty miles of distance between Round Island and the present camp required five days to accomplish. A dozen or more rapids, of all descriptions, had to be passed; some were violent and deep, others shallow. At a few the bed of the stream was sandy; but generally it was composed of gravel and pebbles. Below the crest of one rapid the current forked, forming two eddies. Several attempts were made to ascend; but the bow was not pointed exactly towards the centre of the fork, and, being thrown off by the eddy, the boat would go down stream, whirling around like a teetotum.[33]

They reached Black Canyon, but a frustrated and increasingly cautious Ives finally sent the *Explorer* back downriver. Ives then led a party overland to the Grand Canyon. After returning from his combined explorations over water and land, he wrote a report of his discoveries, expressing his opinion that the region of the Colorado held no value for further exploration. His analysis of the lower Colorado region was grim and matter-of-fact, offering no hope for the future of the lands of the Southwest:

> The region last explored is, of course, altogether valueless. It can be approached only from the south, and after entering it there is nothing to do but leave. Ours has been the first, and will doubtless be the last, party of whites to visit this profitless locality. It seems intended by nature that the Colorado River, along the greater portion of its lone and majestic way, shall be forever unvisited and undisturbed.[34]

At the time, Ives's conclusions about the lands surrounding the lower Colorado River seemed indisputable. The harshness of the landscape and the desolate nature of the arid, inhospitable lands that surrounded the Colorado River's courses seemed to doom the river to purposeless obscurity. His own explorations led him to determine that the great southwestern river was nearly unnavigable and could only be approached from the south. Anyone who might attempt a voyage down the Colorado from its upper reaches would face the fury of its treacherous rapids.

Ives's career as an explorer was cut short by the Civil War. In 1861, he joined the Confederate army and was killed in battle. He did not live long enough to see his prediction of the future uselessness of the Colorado River region proven wrong. Less than a decade after his death, however, another Colorado River explorer would not only prove Ives wrong, he would do it in such a way as to be remembered as one of the most intrepid of all American river explorers.

As late as the mid-nineteenth century, the Colorado had not been fully explored, much less mapped or surveyed. It was still a river of mystery and rumor. Much of the mystery and myth of the Colorado River was soon illuminated by an intrepid government surveyor named John Wesley Powell. Powell was a skilled scientist and explorer and had just the right combination of qualities and talents to provide more information about the Colorado in one decade than had been amassed during the previous 300 years. Because of his explorations down the Colorado during the 1860s and 70s and the official government reports he compiled about his travels, Powell would one day become one of the most lauded and recognized authorities on the river and its canyon lands. No one before or since has lured more Americans to the area.

John Wesley Powell was born an easterner, yet his life seemed always pointed toward the West. He was born in 1834 near Mount Morris, New York. The Powells moved several times during John Wesley's formative years, living in Wisconsin, then Ohio, and finally Illinois, where young Powell spent most of his childhood. His father earned a living as a farmer and by preaching on the side as a Methodist minister. Growing up, young John worked hard on the family farm and developed a love of the outdoors. At an early age, "he acquired an abiding love of practical natural science."[35] Although his formal education as a youth was limited, Powell, at age 18, became a teacher in a country schoolhouse. Largely self-taught, he studied hard just to stay ahead of his students, borrowing books from the library of a family with whom he boarded.

Throughout the 1850s, Powell taught himself everything he could about geology. Between semesters, when he was not teaching, he often took long river trips, floating down the Ohio, the Illinois, and the Des Moines, gathering natural specimens and geological curiosities. He even managed to complete a downriver voyage of every mile of the Mississippi from St. Paul to New Orleans. During these same years, Powell gained a reputation as a naturalist and became the secretary of the Illinois Natural History Society. He also became a noted speaker on natural history. His father had traveled as a circuit-riding minister; young John Wesley followed a similar circuit through Tennessee, Kentucky, and Mississippi, but his subject of choice was natural history, not the supernatural.

In 1861, the year that the bloody war between Northern and Southern states began, John Wesley Powell enlisted in the Union army as a private. Powell's induction record reveals a youth who was "age 27, height 5'6 1/2" tall, light complected, gray eyes, auburn hair." [36] Powell's wartime service resulted in a quick advance to the rank of lieutenant, then to captain of artillery. Despite his military responsibilities, Powell found time to marry his cousin, Emma Dean, during a furlough in November of 1861.

It was during the spring of 1862, on the battlefield at Shiloh, Tennessee, that artillery commander Powell was seriously wounded by a musket ball after raising his right arm to signal to his cannoneers to open fire. The lead ball "plowed up his arm almost to the elbow." [37] The wound was so severe it required the amputation of Powell's arm just below the elbow. Despite his handicap, Powell remained in uniform until the war was over; he was even promoted to major. Powell refused to allow the loss of his arm to end his military service. While still in uniform, he maintained his interest in geology. During field inspections of earthen fortifications and redoubts, Powell would often pick up rock samples and fossil specimens, some of which were later added to museum collections.

After the war, Powell took up serious study, achieving a position as professor of natural history at several Illinois colleges. Powell's work led to the establishment of a natural history museum in Bloomington, Illinois. While serving as the museum's director, Powell received authorization to take a trip out West, where he was to collect rock specimens from the Rocky Mountains. When funds for the expedition proved inadequate, Powell gained additional support from several railroad companies, including the Union Pacific and the Chicago and Rock Island. During a trip to Washington, D.C., the young geologist rustled up old army wagons from the War Department. The Smithsonian Institution provided him with scientific instruments in exchange for Powell's promise to provide the institution with all his scientific data and any maps he produced of the Colorado River system. President Ulysses S. Grant, Powell's commander during the Shiloh and Vicksburg campaigns, gave Powell additional support, "which took the form of an authorization to draw rations at cost from western army posts and the assistance of an army escort out of Fort Laramie." [38]

By early June 1867, Powell was ready to set off on his exploration of the Colorado River region. He traveled west in the company of several of his own natural history students, several interested friends, and a few relatives, including his wife, Emma. That summer, the group hiked the rugged mountain country of the Colorado Rockies, including Pike's Peak, collecting specimens for the Illinois Natural History Society. After a successful expedition, Powell mounted another during the summer of 1868, taking two dozen students into the central Colorado wilderness. His party searched for geological specimens on the summit of 14,000-foot Long's Peak. After two successful land explorations in Colorado, Powell's interest turned toward the region's mountain waterways, including the Grand and Colorado Rivers.

Through the winter of 1868–1869, Professor Powell gathered financial support from government and private sources. Despite such support, Powell provided much of his party's support out of his own pocket. He oversaw the construction of specially designed boats for navigating the Colorado and Green rivers. Three of the boats were 21 feet in length. They were made of oak, and "divided into three compartments, the two on the ends decked to form watertight cabins." [39] Powell hoped the watertight cabins would help keep the boats afloat in the Colorado's rapids, "should the waves roll over them in rough water." [40] The fourth boat was a smaller and lighter model. Crafted from pine, it was designed for rowing. This boat was named the *Emma Dean*, in honor of Powell's wife, and Powell served as its commander. It was in these four untried river vessels that John Wesley Powell intended to take his party down the Colorado's length, "from the cradle of the Rocky Mountains to the Pacific Ocean." [41]

By May of 1869, Powell, his party of river explorers, and their boats were ready. The group had stowed away ten months of rations for the great unknown voyage that lay ahead of them. In addition, the explorers had packed away a variety of tools that could be used to make boat repairs when needed. They also brought along several guns for hunting and protection from wild animals, as well as potentially hostile Indians. Several of his river crew had accompanied Powell on his earlier voyages, but he was the only scientist among them. He was careful to take a variety of scientific instruments along on the downriver exploration to record important information and data. Most of those who signed on for the trip were friends of the famous geologist, men semiskilled at best in boat handling and in the art of wilderness survival. On May 24, Powell's expedition, comprising four newly constructed boats and ten companions, was ready to set out on the river. As Powell would later describe the scene, "The good people of Green River City turn out to see us start. We raise our little flag, push the boats from shore, and the swift current carries us down."[42] For some of the men, it was to be a fateful voyage. Before it was all over, three of the ten would be killed.

5

The "Great Unknown"

After assembling at Green River, Wyoming, John Wesley Powell and his party embarked down the Green River and found the first 60 miles easy going. There were no difficult rapids, and this allowed them to get a feel for how their boats would handle as they descended the river. They were put to the test on their first day on the river when a swift current ran one of the boats onto a rock, breaking an oar and capsizing with its occupants. After two days on the river, the four-boat party reached "a flaring, brilliant, red gorge, that may be seen from the north a score of miles away."[43] Powell named the canyon Flaming Gorge. Here, the party engaged in three days of scientific study, measuring the gorge walls, which towered 1,200 feet above the river, and taking weather readings.

Shortly after they returned to the river, they faced their first serious challenge. At a gorge known today as Hideout Canyon (part of what Powell named "Horseshoe Canyon") the boats hit a curving rapid where the water poured violently over a scattering of jagged rocks. As the ten men and four boats maneuvered the rapid, the party experienced both an exhilarated excitement and a good bit of nervous fear. After their first week on the river, Powell's expedition reached a broad part of the river and a high dome of rock that was honeycombed with thousands of holes occupied by swallows' nests. Powell named the site Beehive Point.

As the party progressed, they passed the border of Wyoming and entered Utah, finding themselves in a great, wide canyon, one of the most spectacular gorges found on the Green River. The cliff walls "were close to a half mile high, stepping backward in terraces."[44] Powell named the gorge Red Canyon. Here, on June 1, the expedition encountered violent rapids. Powell later described them as "an exciting ride."[45] While camping in the canyon, Powell's men discovered a high rock on a trail that featured an inscription left by an earlier explorer of the Green River, William Ashley. It was a modest written record left behind by the famous mountain man and fur trapper more than a generation earlier and read simply "Ashley, 1825."

After two weeks on the Green River, the Powell party finally reached the confluence of the Green and Colorado Rivers. There, at Lodore Canyon, located southeast of the tricorner where Wyoming, Utah, and Colorado join, the men experienced a significant loss. While maneuvering rapids in "a hellish sluice-way,"[46] one of the heavy boats crashed into a series of rocks. The craft broke up and its cargo was lost. Fortunately, the men onboard survived and were rescued. As Powell recorded later, "Down the river half a mile we find . . . the wrecked boat, with a part of the bottom, raged and splintered. . . . There are valuable articles in the cabin; but . . . we determine that life should not be risked to save them. Of course, the cargo of rations, instruments, and clothing is gone."[47]

The loss of this boat meant the loss of a third of their food rations and several articles of extra clothing. After a difficult night of assessing their losses, two of Powell's men finally volunteered to try and reach the smashed boat and salvage all the contents they could. They managed to rescue a package of thermometers and a keg of whiskey that the men had hidden on the boat without Powell's knowledge. Powell took the surprise good-naturedly.

This serious accident was a sobering experience for everyone. One of the party, an Englishman named Frank Goodman, would soon announce he was leaving the expedition, having "seen danger enough."[48] The endless cycle of roiling rapids had already shaken all the men. With the loss of one of his boats and the departure of one of his crew, Powell even considered abandoning his plans to navigate the Colorado River. No one—not even William Ashley—had ever traveled this far downriver. In a private letter, Powell expressed his concerns. Sitting on the rim of a canyon towering 2,000 feet above the river, his feet dangling over the edge, Powell penned: "[Below] is the gateway through which we enter [on] our voyage of exploration . . . and what shall we find?"[49]

As the nine remaining explorers continued down the Green River, they faced additional problems. Ironically, the long gaps

In 1869, Major John Wesley Powell, shown here with a Native-American guide, led the first of many explorations of the Colorado River. Powell was rewarded for his surveys of the Colorado River by being named director of the U.S. Geological Survey by the U.S. government in 1881.

between threatening rapids, where the river ran placid for mile after mile, were extremely boring. On occasion, Powell would try to break up the monotony by reading aloud to his men from such classics as Sir Walter Scott's *Marmion* and *Lady of the Lake*. The challenges of rapids, potentially lurking around each bend in the river, remained a danger. One of Powell's men described paddling the rapids as "like sparking a black-eyed girl—just dangerous enough to be exciting."[50] The constant moisture spoiled their foods and kept their clothes damp at all times. Some of the men gave up on clothes and wore nothing but their longjohns. Powell did not let wet clothes bother him, choosing sometimes to wear none at all. As one of his companions later wrote, "Major Powell said he was dressed when he had his life preserver on."[51]

By the first week of July, the party of nine set out on the second leg of their exploration. Every mile they floated, they were in previously unknown territory. They floated to the mouth of the White River then reached the Uinta Valley. There, the walls of the river canyons began to rise higher around them as the surrounding valley lands disappeared from their river-bound view. Rapids and cataracts continued to plague their progress, and they faced "canyons [that] are very tortuous."[52]

Not only did Powell face the continuous challenge of the turbulent waters of the Green's canyons, but also he was constantly lured up the cliff sides themselves, scaling canyon walls with only one arm. On one occasion, he found himself stranded on a high cliff with no visible way to go back down or continue upward. Holding onto the side of the sheer cliff with his good arm, "his muscles began to quake and his grip was failing fast."[53] He was rescued by one of his men who removed and threw down to Powell the only article of clothing he had on—his longjohns. With these, he managed to pull the major to relative safety.

When the men and their three boats reached the juncture of the Green and Grand rivers, they had been on the river for two months. The food they had started with was spoiled, and what was left would not last them more than two months, even if there was no more spoilage. On July 21, they arrived at the confluence of the Green and the Colorado, a milestone that restored their confidence and strengthened them. At last, they were on the great river itself, its southwesterly flow "wide and deep and the color of cocoa."[54] As they pushed downriver, they soon reached one of the most awesome sights of their expedition: a beautiful, geological wonder of a canyon featuring great, ancient monoliths of sandstone rising hundreds of feet above the river. Water-streaked walls decorated the canyon with ribbons of contrasting colors. Powell was later moved to record the sights as his boats glided downriver:

> Past these towering monuments, past these mounded billows of orange sandstone, past these oak-set glens, past these fern-decked alcoves, past these mural curves, we glide hour after hour, stopping now and then, as our attention is arrested by some new wonder.[55]

Although these sandstone monoliths first led Powell to name the fantastical gorge Monument Canyon, he later changed the name:

> On the walls, and back many miles into the country, numbers of monument-shaped buttes are observed. So we have a curious ensemble of wonderful features—carved walls, royal arches, glens, alcove gulches, mounds, and monuments. From which of these features shall we select a name? We decided to call it Glen Canyon.[56]

For nearly 150 miles, Glen Canyon lured the men downriver. There they found some peace. The waters of the river were relatively still; there were none of the relentless rapids they had battled in the previous weeks. Despite the peacefulness of the canyon's waters, they were distracted by other troubles. Their food supply was miserably low and there seemed little hope of finding enough food to continue their journey much farther. Powell pressed on, however, and by late July, their three boats reached the confluence of the San Juan and Colorado rivers. The surging waters of the San Juan entered the Colorado from the left and joined its muddy stream with the main river, creating a great drainage that caught up the three boats. Augmented by the San Juan, the Colorado was a massive flow of dark, muddy water.

By August 9, Powell's boats reached a deep canyon, its walls flanking the Colorado to a height of 2,500 feet. The walls were "of marble, of many beautiful colors, often polished by the waves."[57] The major walked along the cliff top, later claiming to have covered a mile across a "marble pavement."[58] The gorge was aptly named Marble Canyon. From this location, the Powell expedition was only days away from the intimidating courses of the Grand Canyon, an extent of the river known only in legend since the days that Spaniards stood on its rim and looked down with wonder at the chasm below. After continuing downriver through additional gorges, the party stopped on the river for a couple of days to dry out their clothing and food and repair their boats so that they would be in good condition before entering the great canyon.

As prepared as they could possibly be, on August 13, Major Powell's men entered the Colorado waters that flowed directly into the Grand Canyon. In his writing, Powell referred to the forbidding canyon as "the Great Unknown."[59] To keep the boats together, the men lashed them to each other, causing the battered watercraft to constantly bang into one another. Because most of the cargo the men had originally set out with was gone, the food having been consumed and other items lost, the boats sat high in the water. Almost instantly, the Powell expedition was dwarfed by the sheer mountain walls of the Grand Canyon, which rose three quarters of a mile above the river. From the canyon's rim, the river had the appearance of a long, twisting brown ribbon of water. The water ran swift, churning "its angry waves against the walls and cliffs that rise to the world above us."[60]

The battered wooden boats ran six miles in half an hour as the narrow canyon stream swept the Powell party along. Another five miles of rapids followed. The day proved exhausting for the men, who had already maneuvered more rapids during the previous ten weeks than they could remember. The next day, the expedition reached an even narrower portion of the Grand Canyon, an area with swift currents. Above, on the canyon walls, rock spires, pinnacles, and crags hugged the cliff side. With each passing mile, the canyon seemed to rise higher. Then, around 11:00 A.M., Powell and his men began to hear a great noise, louder than the rush of the rapids. Cautiously, the explorers approached the noise, which grew louder and louder, until they reached "a long, broken fall, with ledges and pinnacles of rock obstructing the river."[61] In less than a third of a mile of the river, the surging stream dropped 80 feet. Massive waves struck the boats, further drenching the already soaked men.

With no way of turning back, the Powell party entered the watery maelstrom. The major later wrote of their experience:

> We strike a glassy wave and ride to its top, down again into the trough, up again on a higher wave, and down and up on waves higher and still higher until we strike one just as it curls back, and a breaker rolls over our little boat. Still onward we speed, shooting past projecting rocks. Hurled back from the rocks now on this side, now on that, we are carried into an eddy, in which we struggle for a few minutes, and are then carried out again, the breakers still rolling over us. Our boat is unmanageable, and we drift another hundred yards through the breakers—how, we scarcely know.[62]

Somehow, Powell and the others successfully floated the destructive waters of yet another Grand Canyon rapid. There, deep in the gloomy gorge, the crash of the rushing waters reverberated off the canyon walls, raising a constant roar of foamy whitewater. Powell and his party knew they were making history as the first humans to attempt a purposeful run through the grandest of all canyons.

During the following days, the party faced the river rapids and rains that slowed their progress, sometimes allowing them to cover only two miles from sunrise to sundown. By August 20, after they had spent a week in the deep gorge, the canyon began to change for the men. The river broadened and the black-slate walls gradually widened. The Powell party began to make great progress. On August 25, their boats floated more than 35 miles. Two days later, however, the men and their boats reached some of the worst rapids yet. An examination of the river revealed to Powell "that lateral streams have washed boulders into the river so as to form a dam, over which the water makes a broken fall of 18 or 20 feet."[63] As the small fleet of boats entered the rapids, the men onboard were certain of their fate. As one of them wrote, "The water dashes against the left bank and then is thrown furiously back against the right. The billows are huge and I fear our boats could not ride them. The spectacle is appalling."[64]

That evening, with the specter of facing another seemingly insurmountable set of rapids the following day looming, three of Powell's men announced that they had had enough of the river and would proceed no farther. They departed the following morning. That morning, Powell named the site of the whitewater run Separation Rapid. The next day, Powell's remaining party hit the river at noon, facing a series of rapids with "no serious difficulty."[65] The men recognized this portion of the Grand Canyon as Grand Wash. They had completed their journey through the unknown portion of the great canyon. The three members of the party who had left them at Separation Rapid had departed just a day too soon.

On August 29, the ragged, ill-fed, and drenched party finally emerged from the Grand Canyon, rejoicing that the worst of the Colorado River was behind them. As Powell later wrote, the "relief from danger, and the joy of success, are great."[66] The Grand Canyon had proven to be a double-edged experience. The marvels of the canyon were constant, the geology an endless source of wonder and fascination. On the other hand, every day spent in the difficult waters of the deepest canyon in the world had caused the men to face danger and the threat of death. "Every waking hour passed in the Grand Canyon," Powell wrote, "[had] been one of toil."[67]

Here the expedition ended. There was no reason for Powell to continue farther down river because the Lower Colorado had already been explored by others. Even steamboats had already plied up and down those lower reaches of the river; no further exploration was needed. As the men sat along the banks of the Colorado, the river that had proven treacherous beyond their imaginations, Powell noted how "the river rolls by us in silent majesty. . . . We sit till long after midnight talking of the Grand Canyon, talking of home."[68]

More than three decades after his final voyage down the Colorado River, Powell summed up what he had learned of the river and its grandest canyon:

> The glories and the beauties of form, of color and sound unite in the Grand Canyon—form unrivaled even by the mountains, colors that view with the sunsets, and sounds that span the diapason from tempest to tinkling raindrop, from cataract to bubbling fountain.[69]

Major John Wesley Powell emerged from his summer exploring the Colorado River as a heroic legend. Newspapers wasted little time telling the story of the one-armed Civil War veteran's successful run on the river. His success was marred only by the news that the three members of his party who had abandoned the exploration prematurely had been killed by Shivwit Indians. Powell hit the lecture circuit and soon made enough money to finance another expedition. In addition, Congress, inspired by Powell's singular success in 1869, appropriated $44,000 for further study of the Colorado.

Over the next eight years, from 1869 to 1877, Powell organized multiple explorations of the Colorado River. One of his chief responsibilities was to complete an accurate survey of the river valley and its endless canyons and peripheral streams. His 1871 voyage downriver was, perhaps, his greatest, "an enterprise far better financed and equipped and with a better quotient of scientific expertise than the first."[70]

Once Powell completed his studies on the river, he was rewarded by the U.S. government and named as director of the U.S. Geological Survey, a post he held for 14 years. Underscoring Powell's achievements on the Colorado is one simple fact. During the 80 years following his successful voyage of exploration down the mysterious red river, only 100 people even attempted to follow in his path by floating the Colorado's full length. He had discovered the nature and beauty and raw violence of a river that had never been fully known. After Powell, the Colorado River would never be looked at in the same way.

6

A River
Out of Control

Powell's explorations of the Colorado during the 1860s and 1870s led others to follow in his wake. Powell's ventures down river were about exploration for its own sake and for the purpose of gathering scientific information, but other explorers examined the river with the intent of making money. In 1889, Frank M. Brown, the president of the newly formed Denver, Colorado Canyon, and Pacific Railroad, tried to sell investors on his plan to build a railroad along the banks of the Colorado River. Skeptics said that the idea was foolhardy and logistically impossible. Brown set out to prove them wrong.

That spring, he organized the Denver, Colorado Canyon, and Pacific Railroad Survey to take the measure of the river and prove that a railroad could be laid along the river's basin. In late March, a small party that included Brown started downriver from Colorado Junction, Colorado. The exploration and survey project that followed did not go well. Within two months, the turbulent waters of the river destroyed 1,200 pounds of the group's stored food supply. By early June, "all provisions had been lost and eight of the expedition's sixteen members had deserted."[71]

When the party reached Lee's Ferry, just down river from Glen Canyon, fresh supplies were purchased and the remaining members of the group continued their hapless float down the turbulent Colorado. Tragedy struck at Marble Canyon, where the boat that President Brown was riding in capsized in the midst of a great whirlpool, causing his death. His body was never recovered or even seen again. For a brief time, the group continued downriver, but they soon gave up, their number having been reduced to four people as others either deserted or drowned. The mission to prove the possibilities of a Colorado River railroad was a failure.

Other explorations of the Colorado continued into the twentieth century. In 1902, the government organized the first expedition to create a topographic map of the Grand Canyon for the United States Geological Survey. The project took place over the next 20 years. By that time, not only had the Geological Survey completed an exact map of the Grand Canyon, the government men also had completed a survey of the entire Colorado River.

During the final decades of the nineteenth century and the early years of the twentieth, many Americans began to eye the Colorado River Basin for its potential as a great source of water for irrigation. As millions of Americans moved west during the three decades following the Civil War, farming across the Great Plains and even in the mountain regions of the Rockies had become extensive and profitable. Questions remained concerning the possibilities of extensive agriculture in the Southwest. John Powell weighed in on the subject in a government document he wrote in 1878, *Report on the Lands of the Arid Regions of the United States*. In the report, Powell stated, "Within the Arid Region only a small portion of the country is irrigable."[72] He declared that there was not enough regular rainfall in the region to raise more crops and declared the importance of irrigation to any future farming in the Southwest. "The question . . . is to devise some practical means by which water rights may be distributed among individual farmers and water monopolies prevented."[73]

Those who wanted to bring farming to the Colorado River Basin remained adamant about developing irrigation systems to facilitate extensive agriculture. As one proponent suggested, the Southwest could become the home of "a million forty-acre farms." In 1902, persuaded by extensive lobbying, the U.S. Congress passed the Newlands Act, which created the Reclamation Service. Under the terms of the act, no one was to receive more water than was needed to irrigate 160 acres of southwestern property, the same number of acres that had been distributed under the government's Homestead Act 40 years earlier.

Even before the 1902 passage of the Newlands Act, investors and schemers had begun developing irrigation systems in the Southwest, using the Colorado River as their water source. In

The Colorado River cuts through Marble Canyon in north-central Arizona. In 1889, Frank M. Brown, president of the Denver, Colorado Canyon, and Pacific Railroad, organized an expedition to prove that a railroad could be set up along the Colorado River's basin. Unfortunately, Brown drowned at Marble Canyon after the boat he was riding in capsized.

1896, entrepreneurs formed the California Development Company, with designs to divert Colorado River water into southern California. By 1898, a wealthy civil engineer and irrigation expert named George M. Chaffey became the company's president. With $150,000 in financial backing, he announced his intention to deliver 400,000 acre-feet of water to the fertile lands of California's Imperial Valley. By 1900, construction was underway for a primary water canal from the Colorado River into the valley, a region inhabited by fewer than 2,000 permanent residents. Six months later, water was being delivered. The California Development Company created a second company, the Imperial Land Company, intending to sell land to thousands of people whom the entrepreneurs expected to flock to 100,000 acres of the newly watered valley.

Irrigation only proved what investors in the California Development Company had always hoped for—that the Imperial Valley could become an oasis and garden in the desert. Critics, including government agents with the U.S. Department of Agriculture, suggested that the valley's soil was so alkaline that it could produce little but "date palms, sorghum and sugar beets." They could not have been more wrong. The silt-rich valley land "produced six cuttings of alfalfa a year, long-staple Egyptian cotton yielding better than a bale to the acre, and grapes and melons maturing earlier than had ever been known."[74]

Soon, Imperial Valley was filling up with people. By 1903, it was home to 7,000 residents, and an additional 3,000 joined them the following year. The Southern Pacific Railroad built a line into the valley, delivering new farmers and their families and hauling out the agricultural abundance.

It seemed that the investors in the California Development Company had hit upon the most reasonable and profitable means of turning the Imperial Valley into a successful farming region. The waters of the Colorado had finally been tapped for profit and were helping encourage the development of southern California. As the Colorado delivered water to a thirsty valley and the population that was growing every day, it was also delivering something the designers of the great diversion canal across the desert had not considered: silt.

The silt that had flowed within the waters of the Colorado for countless millennia was beginning to accumulate to the point of clogging up the canal. The amount of silt entering the canal each day of its use was enough "to build a levee 20 feet high, 20 feet wide, and a mile long."[75] Only two years after the completion of the Imperial Canal, silt had filled it up just four miles from where it connected with the Colorado. Suddenly, the dreams of thousands of new residents of southern California were drying up. The canal could not longer be used, the California Development Company had no funds or equipment to dredge it out, and crops across the Imperial Valley were scorching under the blistering sun of the California desert.

As farmers in the valley began threatening the California Development Company with lawsuits and other claims, company officials were desperate for answers. A new company president, Anthony K. Heber, gave orders to his engineers to have the canal's opening enlarged by dynamiting. His chief engineer protested, "frightened lest he lose control of the river."[76] After lengthy examination of the problem, it was determined that a new intake for the canal would be dug, located "in the soft earth four miles below the Mexican boundary."[77] President Heber negotiated with Mexico's President Porfirio Díaz for permission to divert Colorado River water across northern Mexican territory. By October of 1904, an agreement was reached and the new intake was cut. All might have gone well and the problem of restarting the major irrigation project in southern California might have been solved except for an unforeseen weather change.

The site of the new intake off the Colorado River had been selected because winter flooding was rare at that point, having only occurred three times in the previous 27 years. That year, however, the winter overflow in the Colorado was enormous, causing the newly opened intake to break its walls as "water tore through [the] Imperial Canal to Mexico and then north into the valley by way of the old Alamo Channel."[78] Soon, immense tides of floodwaters poured into Mexico's Volcano Lake, filling it to overflowing. When that lake flooded, the diverted Colorado waters created a new channel, which came to be known as New River, and began flooding the farm fields of Imperial Valley.

For months, the Colorado relentlessly flooded the valley. Engineers for the California Development Company tried to create a "60-foot dam of piles, brush and sandbags,"[79] but their efforts were unsuccessful. By the summer of 1905, the intake off the Colorado had further collapsed. It had widened to 160 feet, allowing the Colorado to flood out at the rate of 90,000 cubic feet per second. As water searched for a low point in California's topography, it found an ancient sink and created a vast inland lake called the Salton Sea.

A desperate President Heber, short on funds to stop the overflow of the Colorado River, appealed to E. H. Harriman, the president of the Southern Pacific Railroad that served Imperial Valley. In some places, the floodwaters had already covered the tracks of the railroad into the valley. Harriman agreed to lend Heber $200,000 but with serious strings attached. He demanded that he be given the power to name a new president to the California Development Company and two of its board of directors. Heber had no choice but to accept the difficult terms. What Harriman did not know at the time was that his $200,000 investment in stemming the irresistible tide of the Colorado River into southern California would prove to be only the beginning.

As engineers looked at the problem of the floodwaters, they decided to build a 600-foot barrier dam at a cost of $60,000, but even as they ordered the construction, nature continued to work against them. By late November, the dam was completed, but a giant flashflood tore down the Gila River, causing floodwaters to rise "10 feet in 10 hours" at Yuma, Arizona. The dam had decreased the Colorado's discharge to 12,000 cubic feet per second; suddenly, the discharge soared to 115,000 feet per second and the entire dam was swept away. By then, Salton Sea already covered 150 square miles of southern California.

At the heart of the problem were two fixed circumstances that competed against one another: Imperial Valley needed the water of the Colorado River to irrigate its fields; however, it did not need as much water as the river was delivering. Engineers hit on a new plan of action. They delivered a powerful steam dredge to the California Development Company's silted canal, intent on excavating the silt out of the first four miles of the man-made waterway. There, they planned to install a massive steel and concrete headgate.

Even as the orders were made for the delivery of the dredge from San Francisco, however, another force of nature thwarted these new plans. In April of 1906, the northern California city was hit by a devastating earthquake and subsequent fire. E. A. Harriman

> . . . sat looking out upon a city wrecked and blackened, almost completely destroyed, then back on his desk to the enormous demands being made upon the Southern Pacific for relief and reconstruction. . . . [In the meantime], the late-spring flood of the Colorado was approaching maximum. . . . In the ruins of San Francisco, Harriman . . . made up his mind. He would advance another $250,000 to check the Colorado.[80]

The river seemed unstoppable. The opening in its banks had reached a half-mile in width and the river was delivering an unfathomable amount of water to California, equal to 6 billion cubic feet every day. Salton Sea was getting longer and deeper (seven inches deeper each day), now covering 400 square miles. Towns in Mexico had already been swept away. Tens of thousands of Californians and Mexicans were in jeopardy of losing their homes and farms.

New engineers were hired. By the summer of 1906, the winter

floods had run their course; in August, another attempt was made to rechannel the waters of the Colorado:

> A huge brush mattress 100 feet wide, sewed with galvanized-iron rope to 3/4-inch cables, was woven and sunk to the bottom of the river, reaching from shore to shore. A pile trestle was built across the crevasse, and over it were run 300 side-dump railroad cars called 'battleships,' each with 60 tons of rock. These were dumped on the brush mattress. . . . All the rock from quarries within a 400-mile radius was commanded.[81]

With laborers in short supply in the deserts of the Southwest, hundreds of Mexican peasant workers were recruited to provide the backbreaking hand labor. In addition, six Indian tribes in the region, the Pima, Papago, Maricopa and Yuma of Arizona and the Cocopah and Diegueno of southern California provided 2,000 men for the work. By early fall, the project was finished and only one question was on everyone's mind: Would the repairs hold?

The answer came soon and swiftly. On October 11, new floods destroyed most of the newly built dam, sweeping it downriver along with the new headgate that had cost $122,000. Repair efforts made progress against the river over the following month, but by December, floodwaters from the Gila River joined those of the Colorado and tore a new breach in an earthen levee downriver, sending new waters into California. By this time, $2 million had already been spent trying to contain the Colorado River in its natural banks. Most of the money had come from the Southern Pacific Railroad, which had taken over control of the California Development Company. It was a decision that E. A. Harriman had come to regret a year earlier.

Searching for another answer, Harriman appealed to the United States government for money and support. He spoke directly with President Theodore Roosevelt, who agreed to

AN EARLY IRRIGATION DREAM FAILS

Although the Colorado River was not tapped extensively for irrigation until the first decade of the twentieth century, one of the first Americans to become convinced the great river could water the desert lands of the region proved to be 40 years ahead of his time.

During the California Gold Rush of the late 1840s, Oliver Meredith Wozencraft, a doctor from New Orleans, loaded up his wife and three children and lit out for the gold camps. As they reached southern California, Wozencraft and his family crossed the Colorado Desert. While crossing this bleak territory, Wozencraft realized that they were moving along the bed of an ancient lake and came to believe that the lakebed lay lower than the Colorado River. After reaching northern California, the doctor hired a surveyor to prove his theory. When it was scientifically determined that the Colorado Desert lay at a lower elevation than the great river, Wozencraft began hammering out a plan to divert the Colorado into the desert.

By 1859, Dr. Wozencraft had become well known in California, taking a role in politics and serving as a delegate to the constitutional convention that helped make California a state. He introduced a bill into the California legislature, requesting ownership of 1,600 square miles of "valueless and horrible desert" on which he promised to deliver water. His next step was to travel to Washington, D.C., to push another bill through Congress. This bill proposed "the introduction of a wholesome supply of fresh water to the Colorado desert."* After years of negotiating his bill through the national legislature, he saw his plan tabled by a committee in 1862 and ignored.

Wozencraft had spent most of his family's money by then and had to hire himself out as a ship's doctor on a Pacific freighter. He never lost his vision of watering the desert of southern California. Years later, he returned to Washington, intent on resurrecting his dream of water in the desert. He and his irrigation plan were scoffed at by members of Congress as "the fantastic folly of an old man." While awaiting yet another introduction of his bill to Congress, Dr. Wozencraft died at the home of a friend, his dream lost—at least for the moment.

* Quoted in Waters, *The Colorado*, 297.

appeal to Congress to "make provision for the equitable distribution of the burden."[82] With assurances from Congress, Harriman ordered nearly all the resources of the Southern Pacific Railroad to be focused on rerouting the unruly waters of the Colorado. By late December, a massive effort was underway. Railroad engineers built two great trestles across the break in the Colorado's banks. Trains were sent in—the entire Los Angeles and Tucson divisions of the railroad were rerouted—delivering immense quantities of rock. Some stone was delivered by rail from as far as 500 miles away. Locomotives delivered pilings and timber from New Orleans. It was a herculean effort: "Never before had rock been dumped so fast . . . 3,000 cars of rock totaling 80,000 cubic yards in 15 days. The whole river was raised bodily 11 feet."[83]

By February 10, 1907, nearly two years after the initial breach in the Colorado River had begun delivering water in abundance to southern California, the great opening was filled and closed. This engineering feat alone cost $1.6 million, but it worked. The Colorado was once again returned to its original channel. For the moment, however, the dream of an endless garden in the desert land of the Imperial Valley had vanished. The Colorado River had "for nearly two years poured unchecked into the valley, destroying farms, homes, communities, and everything in its path."[84] Roads were under water or had otherwise been destroyed. Towns had been swept away. Farm fields and ranches were left to dry under a merciless desert sun. The Southern Railroad had suffered ruinous losses: Between repairing the breach to the Colorado River dam and paying off the claims of American and Mexican settlers, the final bill for taking control of the California Development Company finally amounted to $6 million.

It was not the last time the Imperial Valley would be threatened by such flooding. A few years later, new floodwaters poured through another break in the Colorado's banks, but this time the waters poured across the Mexican landscape, diverted by the various levees that had been built to divert the 1905–1907 floods.

In time, Imperial Valley would recover from the prolonged natural and man-made disasters it had faced during the early years of the twentieth century. A powerful lesson had been learned. Any attempt to tame the Colorado River in the future would have to be made on a scope equal or greater to the power of the river itself.

Today, nearly a century after the great flood of the Colorado into southern California, the waters of the Salton Sea remain, a silent testimony to man's capacity to miscalculate the power of the Colorado River.

7

Taming
the Colorado

Even before the 1905 flooding of the Imperial Valley and southern California's Colorado Desert, the United States government was giving serious attention to the problem of the Colorado's wildness. The main problem was the river's constantly changing nature. It might send floodwaters across a barren lowland of the Southwest during one exceptionally wet spring, and the next year it might remain in its banks, leaving regional farmers high and dry. It was this unreliability, the natural unpredictability of the river, that made life for many in the Southwest, especially farmers, untenable. The river, many thought, had to be tamed.

In 1902, a new office of the federal government, the Bureau of Reclamation was established, and American engineers studied the Colorado River for a site suitable for the construction of a major dam system. During the intervening years, the bureau studied dozens of possible sites. By 1919, they had narrowed their list to two—Boulder Canyon and Black Canyon. (The two canyons stand just 20 miles from one another.) Five more years of study determined the Black Canyon site as the one geologically, hydraulically, and geographically most suitable. A dam would be constructed at Black Canyon, and it would involve a construction project unlike any that had ever preceded it.

Selecting a site for a major dam project had taken years, but site selection was only the beginning of the great tasks that the government project would include. Officials of the federal government had to sit down with officials from the seven states that shared the geography of the Colorado River Basin— Colorado, Utah, Wyoming, Arizona, Nevada, New Mexico, and California—and with representatives of the government of Mexico. Such meetings involved questions of water management and how much water would be allocated to each state. By November of 1922, commissioners from six of the states met in Salt Lake City with then Secretary of Commerce Herbert Hoover (who would be elected president of the United States in 1928). They signed a document called the Colorado River Compact, an agreement that opened the way for the construction of the proposed dam project. (The seventh state, Arizona, refused to sign, convinced that the project would take away some of its rights to the Colorado's water.)

Six years later, the United States Congress passed the Boulder Canyon Project Act. The act provided for additional dams to be constructed. The new design now incorporated plans for the Boulder Dam and the Parker Dam, which would provide water storage for southern California; the Imperial Dam, which would store water for irrigation in the fertile Imperial Valley; the Colorado River Aqueduct, which would reroute water for the general population of southern California; and the All-American Canal, which would ensure complete control of the Colorado by the United States and limit the amount of water allowed to reach Mexico.

Despite the multiple layers of the Boulder Canyon Project Act, the centerpiece of the new legislation was the construction of Boulder Dam. The dam was intended to "store and regulate water delivered to Imperial Reservoir and to Lake Havasu behind Parker Dam."[85] It would provide significant flood protection, and the electricity the hydroelectric generators produced would electrify southern California, Nevada, and Arizona, while providing "energy . . . needed to lift water 1,600 feet from the river's bed over mountains and deserts to the Coastal Plain of Southern California."[86] If Boulder Dam could, indeed, satisfy all those needs, its designers and engineers believed it would stand as one of the greatest water projects in history.

The act also provided the necessary monies—$175 million—for building the various projected dams. Uniquely, the government project was foreseen as partially self-funding. The profits produced from selling electricity could help pay back the cost of construction. (This indeed occurred. By 1976, the government dam system financed by the Boulder Canyon Project Act had grossed $378 million on electricity sales, returning $202 million to the government. Ten years later, the final payment was delivered, making the water reclamation project one of the few self-funding programs in American history.)

As engineers began to develop their plans for the construction of the giant dam to be located at Black Canyon, which nearly straddled the border between Arizona and Nevada, they understood that they were tackling a monumental engineering feat. The walls of Black Canyon

> . . . rose in a sharply vertical angle eight hundred feet above the surging river confined at the base of the canyon. The site was in an unsettled desert wilderness. The nearest railroad was forty miles away at the small village of Las Vegas, Nevada, and the nearest source of sufficient electrical power was 222 miles away at San Bernardino, California. Virtually everything necessary to build the structure—including the labor force— would have to be imported.[87]

Such logistical problems made the task of constructing Hoover Dam formidable; the engineering needed was extremely intricate, requiring more than just building a great wall of concrete to hold back the raging currents of the Colorado River.

Before construction of the dam could even begin, the river had to be diverted from its ancient bed around the dam site. This required the building of four diversion tunnels (each measuring 50 feet in diameter), which would be carved out of solid rock. The tunnels would measure between 3,000 and 4,000 feet in length. Before construction on the tunnels commenced, workers called "cherry pickers" were lowered down the canyon walls. Swinging out on ropes as they dangled 500 feet above the Colorado River, they placed dynamite charges designed to remove any loose rock from the canyon's volcanic rock face. The work was both dangerous and backbreaking.

Construction on the tunnels began with explosive detonations on May 12, 1931. The tunnels that had been designed were so large in circumference that there was no existing equipment to carve them from the hard rock of Black Canyon. Special equipment had to be designed and invented, including a great tunneling drill called the "jumbo," which featured "special multiple rock-drilling rigs mounted on ten-ton trucks with a battery of thirty rock drills mounted onto different platform levels."[88] The trucks were backed up to the tunnels, their 30-bit drill sets pummeling into the hard rock simultaneously, with some of the bits sinking as much as 20 feet into the rock. The drill holes were then filled with explosives and detonated, loosening up more than 2,000 tons of rock at a time. A typical series of coordinated tunnel blasts increased a tunnel by an average of 17 feet. For the men working inside these massive tunnels, the heat was often stifling, reaching as high as 150 degrees. The work on the tunnels required 18 months of exhausting labor.

Then, beginning on the evening of November 12, 1932, dump trucks began delivering loads of rock into the riverbed below the tunnel entrances. This would raise the river by ten feet, causing the mighty waters to flow into the diversion tunnels:

> For fifteen hours, truckload after truckload—one every fifteen seconds—was dumped into the river, and slowly it began to back up against the barrier . . . by 11:30 the next morning, the river had been raised; a blast of dynamite opened the outer tunnel on the Arizona side, another opened the Nevada tunnel, and the river was turned."[89]

The last remaining trickles of river water were then walled off by huge earth-filled cofferdams, both upriver and downriver from the dam site. The site was pumped out, removing all remaining water, and construction could then begin on the dam itself. First, the engineers oversaw the excavation of the site 100 feet below the exposed riverbed until the workers reached bedrock, the only solid foundation the massive dam could rest on. Writer Frank Waters visited the dam site in 1932. In his book *The Colorado*, he recorded the sights he witnessed one starlit night just after midnight:

> The vast chasm seemed a slit through earth and time alike. The rank smell of Mesozoic ooze and primeval muck filled

the air. Thousands of pale lights, like newly lit stars, shone on the heights of the cliffs. Down below grunted and growled prehistoric monsters. . . . They were steam shovels and cranes feeding on the muck, a ton at a gulp. . . . From the walls above shot beams of searchlights, playing over this vast subterranean arena.[90]

By the summer of 1933, that task was completed as the shovels of the great steamers scraped bedrock. Soon, the dam began to rise out of Black Canyon.

During the preparation phase of the actual dam construction, other work was also being completed. Roads were under construction, a town—Boulder City—was erected where there had been only scrubby desert, and the Interior Department gave the green light for the construction of a line of the Union Pacific Railroad from Las Vegas to the dam site. The town was needed to house all the thousands of construction workers required for the construction at Black Canyon. It emerged from the desert floor and featured "paved streets, stores, tidy bungalows and . . . barracks, enormous mess halls, garages, machine and service shops. Telephone and telegraph service were provided."[91] Many houses were furnished with a modern convenience considered rare at the time but necessary for men working in the desert where overnight temperatures often remained above 85 degrees: air conditioning.

The company contracted to accomplish all this construction was in fact a consortium of six large construction firms. Appropriately named Six Companies, the new firm was responsible for building the dam, the tunnels, and the town. At its peak, Six Companies employed more than 5,000 people—everyone from bookkeepers to engineers to truck drivers to dynamiters. As one observer noted, building Hoover Dam required the efforts of "5,000 men in a 4,000-foot canyon."[92]

By early June of 1933, the first loads of concrete had been poured in a unique honeycomb system of chambers that would form the superstructure of Hoover Dam. Giant buckets of concrete were dumped into individual square forms, each containing eight cubic yards. The size of the dam set the pattern for how the dam itself was poured. When finished, the dam was to stand 726 feet in height and stretch across the canyon a distance of more than 1,200 feet. The dam was to be much wider at its base than at its top, the base bulging out to 660 feet in thickness and then tapering to a top that measured a mere 45 feet wide. Engineers estimated the amount of concrete needed to create the basic structure of Hoover Dam at 3.25 million cubic yards. If the entire dam had been poured as a massive solid of concrete, experts calculated it would have required 125 years for the mass of cement to harden completely. Even then, "the enormous pressures exerted on it by its own bulk would have raised the internal temperatures of the concrete to heights capable of warping and cracking it."[93]

For these reasons, the dam was poured "like a gigantic game of children's blocks."[94] Two hundred boxed shafts were built to contain concrete, each technically separate from the others but together forming the ultimately solid mass of the super-sized dam. Each container held a system of refrigerated copper tubing to help facilitate even temperature control as the concrete dried in the heat of the desert. Water chilled to 38 degrees was pumped through the one-inch tubing buried in each block of concrete, allowing the entire mass of concrete to cool, block-by-block, in less than two years. The cooled water was produced by a refrigeration facility equipped with a 3,000-gallon-per-minute cooling tower, capable of producing 1,000 tons of ice daily. In addition to the concrete, 45 million pounds of reinforcing steel were used to strengthen the dam. As the concrete dried and the forms were removed, grout, or liquid concrete, was pumped into the spaces between each column of concrete, bonding all the columns together into a giant monolithic barrier. For nearly two years, an endless stream of buckets of concrete swung out over the slowly rising dam on great, 250-ton-capacity, overhead cable systems. The concrete was delivered to the work site from two concrete mixing plants that churned out concrete around the clock.

The Hoover Dam, situated at Black Canyon, on the border of Arizona and Nevada (30 miles southeast of Las Vegas), was constructed from 1931–1936 to check the wild Colorado River whose unpredictability often led to flooding or lack of water for farmers in the region.

For many of the thousands of men working at the dam site, labor was always hampered by unbearable heat and the danger of working at heights equivalent to being on top of an 80-story

A DAM BY ANY OTHER NAME

Today, any visitor to the giant dam that sits astride the Colorado River in Boulder Canyon knows the massive concrete barrier as the Hoover Dam. For several years, however, the monumental dam went by another name: Boulder Dam. Why the dam went through a change in names remained a mystery for years, but the story behind it is one for the history books.

When Congress passed the Boulder Canyon Project Act in 1928, the general assumption was that the dam slated to be constructed at that site would be named the Boulder Dam. Two years later, at the suggestion of then Secretary of the Interior Ray Lyman Wilber, Congress passed an act declaring that the dam be named after President Herbert Hoover. As secretary of commerce, Hoover had been instrumental in facilitating the creation of the Colorado River Compact, without which the entire dam project would never have been built.

Despite this clear Congressional mandate, in 1935, at the dedication of the dam, the name was quietly changed. In a copy of the speech delivered by President Franklin Roosevelt at the dedication, his secretary of state, Harold Ickes, actually crossed out Hoover's name and wrote in "Boulder." The Republican Hoover, because of the economic depression then sweeping across the United States, had become extremely unpopular with many Americans. The name "Boulder Dam" stuck for more than a decade.

Then, in 1947, President Harry Truman requested that Congress determine the legal and true name of the dam. An investigation revealed that the actual name of the great southwestern dam had always been Hoover. Even today, however, there are those who still refer to the massive water storage facility as Boulder Dam.

To add to the irony of it all, the dam was not even constructed in Boulder Canyon but in Black Canyon, 20 miles downriver from Boulder.

building. These unique conditions made so many of the jobs related to the building of Hoover Dam hazardous:

These extreme temperatures, together with the noise, dust, smoke, and the constant danger from heavy equipment, rocks, and falling debris made accidents an everyday occurrence. A sixty-bed hospital was built in Boulder City to handle cases of heat exhaustion and accidents, and two ambulances were always on standby. At the dam site, first-aid stations were set up that handled as many as 1,500 minor injuries per month. (These hardy workers considered as "minor" almost any injury that did not result in death.)[95]

There were deaths, as well. Between 1931 and 1937, 96 people died during the building of Hoover Dam. Two dozen fell to their deaths, 26 were struck by falling objects, and another 26 died after being hit by heavy equipment. Ten were victims of explosions, five were electrocuted, three drowned, and two others died in elevator or cableway accidents.

As enormous in scope as the great construction project was, Hoover Dam was completed in just five years. During the spring of 1935, the final bucket of concrete was poured. On September 30, during an elaborate dedication ceremony, President Franklin Roosevelt visited the finished dam and delivered his dedicatory address before an enthusiastic crowd of 12,000.

Those who had spent many difficult months working at the Hoover Dam site understood that they had played a part in building one of the most spectacular structures of the twentieth century. As writer Theodore White observed, "From designing engineer to lowest laborer, they are acutely aware of the immensity and importance of the dam. To them, it assumes a personality and they are devoted to it. . . . In each there is a feeling of ownership."[96] Frank Crowe, one of the executive directors of the Six Companies, observed, "There's something peculiarly satisfying about building a great dam. You know that what you build will stand for centuries."[97] The dam soon became a symbol of the engineering capabilities of modern man, a combination of talent, design, and ingenuity that had, after hundreds of thousands of years, tamed the mighty waters of the Colorado River. The river would never be the same.

8

Epilogue

With the completion of the massive Hoover Dam, the modern-day harnessing of the great Colorado River had begun. Within weeks of the dedication of the massive dam in September of 1935, the first of the dam's electricity-producing generators came on line, followed by a second the following month, and a third by year's end. (The seventh, and final, generator at Hoover Dam went into operation more than 25 years later, in 1961.) As for the newly tamed Colorado, the diversion tunnels were closed and the river began to form an immense reservoir of water. Called Lake Mead, this reservoir ultimately stretched 110 miles behind the dam.

Today, Lake Mead has a water storage capacity of more than 32 million acre-feet of water, "enough water to cover the entire state of New York to a depth of one foot."[98] This vast amount of water is equal to the entire average flow of the Colorado over two years. The water of the lake covers several of the timeless canyons once floated by John Wesley Powell.

The dam's hydroelectric generators have remained on line for nearly 70 years and have collectively produced more than 200 billion kilowatts of power, enough to supply a million people for a quarter of a century. Additional dams have been built since the Hoover, adding to the power generating capacity of the river.

Parker Dam, part of the original Colorado River Project, was completed in 1938. Three hundred and twenty feet tall, it is much smaller than the Hoover Dam, but "if [Hoover] Dam was the world's tallest dam, then Parker Dam was the 'deepest,' for excavation crews had to dig down 233 feet before reaching bedrock."[99] Two-thirds of Parker Dam lies below the Colorado River bed.

Lake Havasu, the vast reservoir that filled behind Parker Dam, proved large enough to provide the 1.1 million acre-feet of water needed from the Colorado for the Colorado River Aqueduct. Work on the aqueduct had begun in 1933; it would eventually produce a system of 42 water tunnels designed to pump water from the Colorado over the mountains separating the river from California's coastal plain to provide water to thirsty southern Californians. The aqueduct was completed in 1939, and water soon began to flow into Lake Matthews, nearly 250 miles from Lake Havasu.

Davis Dam, located 67 miles downstream from Black Canyon, was completed in 1951 (the work on Davis was halted in mid-project by World War II). Davis is much smaller than Hoover. It is a 200-foot high, earth-and-rockfill dam that provides electricity for southern Arizona, California, and Nevada, and its reservoir, Lake Mohave, provides the lion's share of Mexico's allotment of the Colorado's water, as delineated in the Mexican Water Treaty of 1944.

Other parts of the Colorado River Project program were completed during the 1930s and 1940s. Imperial Dam was completed in 1938, and the first water from the dam arrived in the Imperial Valley by way of the All-American Canal in October of 1940.

Other dams copied the Hoover, Parker, and Davis models. The Mexican government constructed its own dam, the Morelos, on the Colorado during the mid-1950s. In 1956, construction began on a dam at Glen Canyon, the first under a newly passed act called the Colorado River Storage project. The 700-foot-tall dam was completed and closed its gates in 1963, backing billions of gallons of water into the canyon and covering over the sublime beauty of its ancient walls forever. Today, the dam at Glen Canyon holds back a 200-mile long reservoir containing, on average, 9 trillion gallons of the Colorado River. The reservoir, named Lake Powell after the intrepid explorer John Wesley Powell, holds water largely allocated for the states sharing the upper Colorado basin: Colorado, New Mexico, Utah, and Wyoming. Currently, Lake Powell boasts 1,800 miles of lakeshore and is a mecca for boaters, water-skiers, campers, and fishermen.

The Colorado River is an ancient American river, and its modern-day version has never been more vital to the lives of those millions of people who rely on its water for drinking, sanitation, industry, electricity, and recreation. Nearly all of the river's 5 trillion gallons of water that flows along the Colorado annually is apportioned to one population group or another. Under an 80-year-old agreement, the Colorado has been divided into

The Hoover Dam has seven electricity-producing generators that provide more than 200 billion kilowatts of power a year. Three states—Arizona, California, and Nevada—and several cities, including Los Angeles, use the power supplied by these generators.

two great basins, with approximately half the river's water going to each. The river's upper basin provides water for New Mexico, Wyoming, Colorado, and Utah; Arizona, California, and Nevada receive the water of the Colorado's lower basin.

The Colorado may not be the longest, widest, or most voluminous river in America, but its location in the desert lands of the Southwest, a region where water is an important and precious resource, renders the Colorado among the most controlled and guarded of all American rivers. As Colorado writer Virginia Hopkins noted, "A scarcity of water is the price human beings pay for living in the desert, and as more and more people move to the warm, dry, sunny climate of the Southwest, the problem grows more and more serious."[100] Today, 19 major dams control the allotment of water flowing in the Colorado River.

At many of the dam sites, the lakes created from the waters of the Colorado River are administered by various government agencies and services, among them the National Park Service (NPS). As early as 1936, the NPS was given administrative responsibility of the Boulder Dam Recreation Area. In 1964, President Lyndon Johnson signed a bill reestablishing the old Boulder Dam Recreation Area, which had been expanded in 1947 to include Lake Mohave, as the Lake Mead National Recreation Area. This act also redefined the western boundary of Grand Canyon National Monument by including Shivwits Plateau. In 1974, the recreational area was increased again, this time to include all of Grand Canyon National Monument. Approximately 30 million fishermen, water-skiers, boaters, and other outdoor enthusiasts visit the reservoirs and lakes of the river annually.

The lakes that now dot the route of the Colorado River are not the only avenue of enjoyment river enthusiasts have at their disposal. In the spirit of John Wesley Powell, the Colorado still features many wild runs, giving thousands of people the opportunity to raft the river's remaining rapids.

Although visitors to the Colorado River can enjoy the great southwestern waterway and its man-made lakes in ways no other generation of Americans could, the Colorado is not a paradise on earth. As with other modern-day rivers, the Colorado faces problems. This river's problems, however, are somewhat different from those of other major American waterways, such as the Missouri, Mississippi, or Ohio. Those rivers struggle with unacceptable pollution levels caused by industrial and urban waste. The Colorado, however, continues to face such age-old problems of nature and environment as high temperatures (it is the warmest river in America), as well as a high evaporation rate. The major problem facing the waters of the Colorado today is not pollution but salinization. Because much of the Colorado's lower basin is used to provide irrigation waters, the river is becoming increasingly salty because of saline deposits (left after evaporation) that eventually drain into the Colorado's main current. As dams are constructed along the river, the Colorado increasingly carries less silt and more salt. Between 1917 and 1961, the saline levels of the Colorado tripled. Where farms flourished in the American Southwest nearly a century ago, many of those lands are abandoned salt flats today. The salt content is so high that Mexicans complain that the Colorado is useless to them because its waters render their farmlands infertile.

Throughout the twentieth century, the Colorado River has been increasingly tamed, and governed, its waters officially allocated as the importance of the river as a natural resource in the region of the Southwest has increased. By the mid-1960s, with nearly all its major dams on line, the Colorado became a river of "year-round tranquil flow."[101] By 1968, however, the National Academy of Sciences issued a grim prediction about the river's future, stating in a report that "the Colorado basin is closer than most other basins in the United States to utilizing the last drop of available water for man's needs."[102] Today, so much Colorado River water is used that the river is actually shorter than it was a century ago. Those waters that reach Mexico often fail to reach the Gulf of California, the historical "mouth" of the river. The final 80 miles of the Colorado are "a mere trickle, winding through a delta of marshes, mud flats and dry lakes."[103] This great American river, which originates in the frosty, glacier waters of the Rocky Mountains, ends ignominiously. It peters out in the Sonoran desert, a once-roaring river shrunken to a silty, salty, exhausted stream. The waters of the Colorado have been overworked by an ever-increasing population lured by the mystery and magic of life in the American Southwest.

10–5 MILLION YEARS AGO River capture linking the Ancestral Colorado River and the Hualapai drainage creates the Colorado River of modern times.

20,000 B.C. First humans are recorded to have reached and lived in the Colorado River Basin region.

2500 B.C. Corn is introduced into the diets of Colorado River Basin Indians.

A. D. 100 The Mogollon become first people of the Colorado River Basin to practice systematic agriculture, erect permanent log and earthen homes, and produce pottery.

750 The Anasazi are living in pueblos in the Four Corners region of the Southwest.

1150–1300 The Colorado River Basin becomes home to new Indian culture group, the Hohokam, excellent irrigation engineers.

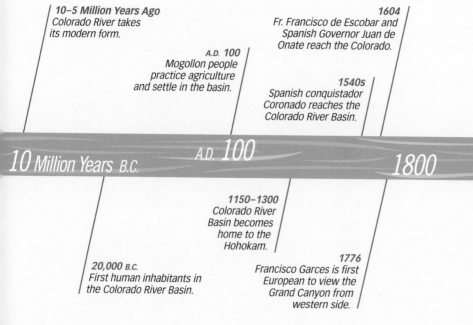

10–5 Million Years Ago
Colorado River takes its modern form.

1604
Fr. Francisco de Escobar and Spanish Governor Juan de Onate reach the Colorado.

A.D. 100
Mogollon people practice agriculture and settle in the basin.

1540s
Spanish conquistador Coronado reaches the Colorado River Basin.

1150–1300
Colorado River Basin becomes home to the Hohokam.

20,000 B.C.
First human inhabitants in the Colorado River Basin.

1776
Francisco Garces is first European to view the Grand Canyon from western side.

10 Million Years B.C.   *A.D. 100*   *1800*

1200s Most Native American residents of the Colorado River Basin either abandon their village complexes or migrate to the river and practice irrigation.

1500s Ancestors of the Hopi and Zuni peoples call the Colorado River their home.

1540s Spanish conquistador Coronado reaches the Colorado River Basin. Some of Coronado's men reach the rim of the Grand Canyon. At the same time, Spanish sea captain Francisco de Ulloa reaches vicinity of the mouth of the Colorado.

1604 Father Francisco de Escobar and Spanish Governor Juan de Onate reach the banks of the Colorado River.

1681 Father Eusebio Francisco Kino establishes mission outpost at the confluence of the Gila and Colorado Rivers.

1825
General William Ashby becomes first white man to float the Colorado.

1826
Lieutenant R.W.H. Hardy enters main channel of Colorado by ship.

1896
Formation of the California Development Company (CDC).

1922
Six U.S. states sign the Colorado River Compact.

1930–1935
Construction of the Hoover Dam.

1825

1900

1975

1869
John Wesley Powell leads a party by boat the length of the Colorado.

1857
U.S. Navy sends Lt. Joseph Christmas Ives by steamboat up the Colorado.

1905–07
Severe flooding destroys the CDC's diversion canal.

1964
President Johnson establishes the Lake Mead Recreation Area.

1744 Father Jacobo Sedelmair floats down the Gila River and reaches the banks of the Colorado.

1761 Jesuit priest Alonso de Posadas reaches the Green River, a major tributary of the Colorado.

1776 Father Francisco Garces becomes first European to view the Grand Canyon from the western side, possibly near El Tovar. That same year, Father Francisco Silvestre Velez de Escalante reaches both the Colorado and Green rivers.

1825 Fur trader General William Ashley becomes the first white man of record to float much of the Colorado River.

1826 British naval officer, Lieutenant R.W.H. Hardy entered the main channel of the Colorado by ship.

1851 First steamboat attempts to steam up the Colorado River from its mouth.

1857 U.S. Navy dispatches Lieutenant Joseph Christmas Ives to command a steamboat up the Colorado. Ives reaches Fort Yuma, the Mojave Canyon, and Black Canyon and walks to Grand Canyon.

1869 John Wesley Powell leads a party by boat along much of the length of the Colorado River.

1889 President of the Denver, Colorado, Canyon, and Pacific Railroad, Frank M. Brown dies on the Colorado trying to take a party downriver to examine the possibilities of building a railroad along the river.

1896 Entrepreneurs form the California Development Company (CDC) and, by 1900, a canal that diverts Colorado River water into Imperial Valley is built.

1902   U.S. Government establishes the Reclamation Service, and that office begins examining a likely location for a major dam on the Colorado River.

1905–7   Severe flooding on the Colorado destroys the CDC's diversion canal, flooding devastates Imperial Valley and Salton Sea is formed from the water flow into southern California.

1922   Representatives from six U.S. states sign the Colorado River Compact, which opens the way for the construction of a Colorado dam.

1930–1935   Hoover Dam is constructed on the Colorado River at Black Canyon.

1938   Parker Dam is completed on the Colorado River; Imperial Dam is completed that same year.

1939   The Colorado River Aqueduct is completed.

1951   Davis Dam is completed on the Colorado River.

1963   Glen Canyon Dam is completed on the Colorado River.

1964   President Lyndon Johnson establishes the "Lake Mead National Recreation Area."

CHAPTER 1

1: Quoted in Ron Redfern, *Corridors of Time: 1,700,000,000 Years of Earth at Grand Canyon* (New York: Times Books, 1980), 40.

2: Quoted in T. H. Watkins, *The Grand Colorado: The Story of a River and Its Canyons* (Palo Alto, CA: American West Publishing Company, 1969), 16.

3: Quoed in Tim McNeese, *Myths of Native America* (New York: Four Walls Eight Windows, 2003), 162.

4: Quoted in Watkins, *Grand Colorado*, 25.

5: Quoted in McNeese, *Myths*, 164.

6: Ibid., 165.

CHAPTER 2

7: Quoted in Frank Waters, *The Colorado* (New York: Rinehart & Company, Inc., 1946), 136.

8: Ibid., 138.

9: Ibid.

10: Quoted in Watkins, *Grand Colorado*, 30.

11: Quoted in Waters, *The Colorado*, 143.

12: Quoted in Watkins, *Grand Colorado*, 32.

13: Quoted in Waters, *The Colorado*, 146.

14: Quoted in Watkins, *Grand Colorado*, 33.

15: Quoted in Robert Wallace, *The Grand Canyon* (Alexandria, VA: TIME-Life Books, 1972).

16: Quoted in Waters, *The Colorado*, 148.

CHAPTER 3

17: Quoted in Watkins, *Grand Colorado*, 37.

18: Ibid.

19: Ibid.

20: Quoted in Waters, *The Colorado*, 153.

21: Quoted in Watkins, *Grand Colorado*, 37.

22: Ibid., 38.

23: Ibid.

24: Ibid.

25: Ibid., 39.

26: Ibid.

27: Quoted in Waters, *The Colorado*, 161.

28: Ibid., 162

CHAPTER 4

29: Quoted in Virginia Hopkins, *Portraits of America: The Colorado River* (Secaucus, NJ: Chartwell Books, Inc., 1985).

30: Quoted in Watkins, *Grand Colorado*, 89.

31: Quoted in Waters, *The Colorado*, 231–32.

32: Quoted in Watkins, *Grand Colorado*, 69.

33: Ibid., 71.

34: Quoted in Hopkins, *Portraits*, 101–2.

35: Quoted in Watkins, *Grand Colorado*, 90.

36: Quoted in John Cooley, *The Great Unknown: The Journals of the Historic First Expedition Down the Colorado River* (Flagstaff, AZ: Northland Publishing, 1988), 6.

37: Ibid.

38: Quoted in Watkins, *Grand Colorado*, 90.

39: Quoted in Waters, *The Colorado*, 243.

40: Quoted in Watkins, *Grand Colorado*, 90.

41: Quoted in Bil Gilbert, *The Trailblazers* (New York: TIME-Life Books), 207.

42: Quoted in Watkins, *Grand Colorado*, 93.

CHAPTER 5

43: Quoted in Watkins, *Grand Colorado*, 95.

44: Ibid., 96.

45: Ibid.

46: Quoted in Gilbert, *The Trailblazers*, 207.

47: Quoted in Watkins, *Grand Colorado*, 99.

48: Quoted in Waters, *The Colorado*, 244.

49: Quoted in Watkins, *Grand Colorado*, 97.

50: Ibid., 99.

51: Quoted in Gilbert, *The Trailblazers*, 209.

52: Quoted in Watkins, *Grand Colorado*, 105.

53: Quoted in Gilbert, *The Trailblazers*, 210.

54: Quoted in Watkins, *Grand Colorado*, 106.

55: Quoted in Cooley, *Great Unknown*, 138.

56: Ibid.

57: Quoted in Wallace, *Grand Canyon*, 125.

58: Ibid.

59: Ibid., 126.

60: Ibid.

61: Ibid., 127.

62: Ibid.

63: Ibid., 128.

64: Quoted in Gilbert, *The Trailblazers,* 210.

65: Quoted in Wallace, *Grand Canyon,* 129.

66: Quoted in Watkins, *Grand Colorado,* 136.

67: Ibid.

68: Quoted in Wallace, *Grand Canyon,* 129.

69: Quoted in Mary Dos-Baba, *The Great Southwest* (New York: Crescent Books, 1985).

70: Quoted in Cooley, *Great Unknown,* 198.

CHAPTER 6

71: Quoted in Watkins, *Grand Colorado,* 141.

72: Ibid., 144.

73: Ibid., 145.

74: Quoted in Waters, *The Colorado,* 299–300.

75: Ibid., 300.

76: Ibid., 301.

77: Ibid.

78: Ibid.

79: Ibid.

80: Ibid., 303.

81: Ibid., 304–5.

82: Ibid., 306.

83: Ibid., 307.

84: Quoted in James C. Maxon, *Lake Mead-Hoover Dam: The Story Behind the Scenery* (Las Vegas, NV: KC Publications, 1980).

CHAPTER 7

85: Quoted in Watkins, *Grand Colorado,* 171.

86: Ibid., 172.

87: Quoted in Maxon, *Lake Mead-Hoover Dam,* 28.

88: Ibid.

89: Quoted in Watkins, *Grand Colorado,* 177.

90: Quoted in Waters, *The Colorado,* 347.

91: Ibid., 345.

92: Ibid., 346.

93: Quoted in Watkins, *Grand Colorado,* 178.

94: Ibid.

95: Quoted in Maxon, *Lake Mead-Hoover Dam,* 29.

96: Quoted in Watkins, *Grand Colorado,* 193.

97: Ibid., 180.

CHAPTER 8: EPILOGUE

98: Quoted in Maxon, *Lake Mead-Hoover Dam,* 30.

99: Quoted in Watkins, *Grand Colorado,* 180.

100: Quoted in Hopkins, *Portraits,* 8.

101: Quoted in Philip L. Fradkin, *A River No More: The Colorado River and the West* (New York: Alfred A. Knopf, 1981), 15.

102: Ibid.

103: Quoted in Hopkins, *Portraits,* 173.

Cooley, John. *The Great Unknown: The Journals of the Historic First Expedition Down the Colorado River.* Flagstaff, AZ: Northland Publishing, 1988.

Dellenbaugh, Frederick S. *The Romance of the Colorado River.* New York: G.P. Putnam's Sons, 1902.

Dos-Baba, Mary. *The Great Southwest.* New York: Crescent Books, 1985.

Dunar, Andrew, and Dennis McBride. *Building Hoover Dam: An Oral History of the Great Depression.* New York: Twayne Publishers, 1993.

Fishbein, Seymour L. *Grand Canyon Country: Its Majesty and its Lore.* Washington, D.C.: National Geographic Society, 1991.

Fleck, Richard F., Ed. *A Colorado River Reader.* Salt Lake City: The University of Utah Press, 2000.

Fletcher, Colin. *River: One Man's Journey down the Colorado, Source to Sea.* New York: Alfred A. Knopf, 1997.

Fradkin, Philip L. *A River No More: The Colorado River and the West.* New York: Alfred A Knopf, 1981.

Hopkins, Virginia. *Portraits of America: The Colorado River.* Secaucus, NJ: Chartwell Books, Inc., 1985.

McNeese, Tim, Ed. *Myths of Native America.* New York: Four Walls Eight Windows, 2003.

Maxon, James C. *Lake Mead-Hoover Dam: The Story Behind the Scenery.* Las Vegas, NV: KC Publications, 1980.

Porter, Eliot. *The Place No One Knew: Glen Canyon on the Colorado.* San Francisco, CA: Sierra Club, 1963.

Pritzker, Barry M. *A Native American Encyclopedia: History, Culture, and Peoples.* New York: Oxford University Press, 2000.

Rawlins, Carol B. *The Colorado River.* New York: Franklin Watts, 1999.

Redfern, Ron. *Corridors of Time: 1,700,000,000 Years of Earth at Grand Canyon.* New York: Times Books, 1980.

Scharff, Robert. *Exploring Grand Canyon National Park.* New York: The World Publishing Company, 1969.

Wallace, Robert. *The Grand Canyon.* Alexandria, VA: TIME-Life Books, 1972.

Waters, Frank. *The Colorado.* New York: Rinehart & Company, Inc., 1946.

Watkins, T. H. *The Grand Colorado:* The Story of a River and Its Canyons. Palo Alto, CA: American West Publishing Company, 1969.

Worster, Donald. *The Life of John Wesley Powell.* New York: Oxford University Press, 2001.

Zwinger, Ann Haymond. Downcanyon: *A Naturalist Explores the Colorado River through the Grand Canyon.* Tucson: The University of Arizona Press, 1995.

INDEX

page:
3: © Amy and Chuck Wiley/Wales/Index Stock Imagery
6: © Amy and Chuck Wiley/Wales/Index Stock Imagery
10: Library of Congress, LC-USZ62-120738
21: © Dave G. Houser/CORBIS

Frontis: Library of Congress, Maps Division
Cover: © CORBIS

29: © Buddy Mays/CORBIS
39: © CORBIS
49: © Bettmann/CORBIS
59: © David Muench/CORBIS
75: © Mark Polott/Index Stock Imagery
81: © Tom Campbell/Index Stock Imagery

ABOUT THE AUTHOR

TIM MCNEESE is an Associate Professor of History at York College in Nebraska. Professor McNeese earned an Associate of Arts degree from York College, a Bachelor of Arts degree in history and political science from Harding University, and a Master of Arts degree in history from Southwest Missouri State University. He is currently in his 27th year of teaching.

Professor McNeese's writing career has earned him a citation in the "Something About the Author" reference work. He is the author of more than fifty books and educational materials on everything from Egyptian pyramids to American Indians. He is married to Beverly McNeese, who teaches English at York College.